Ingrid Bolle-Kleinbub

West Highland White Terr

In collaboration with Christine Metzger

Contents

Preface 3

West Highland White Terriers: Quick and Self-confident 4
The Westie, a "Large" Small Dog 4
The Origin of the Breed 6
The Breed Standard 10
Brief Profile of the Westie 11

When a Westie Joins Your Household 12
Will a Westie Fit Into Your Life? 12
A Male or a Female? 12
A Puppy or a Full-grown Dog? 13
One Westie or Two? 13
Westies and Other Pets 14
Choosing Your Puppy 14
How to Find a Good Breeder 14
Vaccination Certificate, Worming, and Feeding Schedule 15
The Pedigree 17
The Contract of Sale 17
Basic Equipment and Accessories 17
Hazards in Your Home 19

Acclimation and the Westie's Daily Routine 20
Bringing Your New Puppy Home in the Car 20
The First Few Days at Home 20
How-to: Training 22
The First Few Nights 24
Housebreaking 24
How-to: Grooming 26
Westies' Behavior 28
Articulate Language 28
Body Language 28
Vacationing with or without Your Westie? 29
The Aging Westie 30
The Final Trip to the Veterinarian 31
Checklist: Taking Your Westie Along on Vacation 31

Proper Nutrition 32
Appropriate Nutrition 32
The Right Amount of Food and the Right Shape 32
Where and When to Feed Your Westie 32
Commercial Dog Food 33
What to Look for in a Dog Food 34
Drinking Water Is Important 34
Bones for Your Westie 34
Rules for Feeding 35
Home-prepared Meals for Your Dog 35
Feeding an Old Westie 36

Westies like to play—as much and as often as possible. Of course, playing is even more fun if it involves another dog.

Preface

If Your Westie Is Overweight 36
Digestive Upsets 37
How-to: Keeping Your Dog Physically
   Fit 38

What to Do If Your Westie Gets Sick 40
How to Tell Whether Your Dog Is Ill 40
How the Dog Owner Can Help 40
What the Veterinarian Needs to
   Know 42
Preventive Medicine: Immunizations
   and Worming 43
Immunization Schedule 43
Worming Schedule 43
Parasites 44
Aujeszky's Disease 45
Craniomandibular Osteopathy 45
How-to: First Aid 46

Breeding Westies 50
Economics of Breeding 50
Responsibility for Breeding 50
Breeding Regulations 50
The Love Life of a Male Dog 51
The Female in Heat 51
Mating 52
Pregnancy 52
False Pregnancy 52
The Whelping Box 52
Birth 54
The Puppies' Development 55
Feeding the Puppies 55

Showing Your Westie 56
Types of Shows 56
How Dogs Are Judged 56
Getting Ready for the Show Ring 58
Trimming Before a Show 58

Index 60

Useful Books and Magazines 62

Addresses, Important Notes 63

The West Highland white terrier, or Westie for short, is an enormously appealing dog, a pet with which you'll fall permanently in love. Full of life, intelligent, highly courageous, and always ready to carry out tasks in a spirit of fun, the Westie makes an ideal playmate for children and an untiring companion for adults on hikes and walks. To develop all its positive qualities, this sturdy, indomitable terrier needs firm, consistent training and appropriate care. In this Barron's pet owner's manual you will learn all you need to know about purchasing a West Highland white terrier, handling the dog properly, providing it with nutritious foods, and helping it if it gets sick.

How-to pages with vivid illustrations supply a variety of information: training a Westie step by step, advice on daily grooming, and first-aid procedures in case of accidents and injuries. Also described is a program for keeping your dog fit through play and exercise. Do you want your Westie to have puppies? The author—an experienced breeder of Westies—explains what prerequisites must be met, what to expect when the puppies are being born, and what you need to be aware of as they develop. In addition, this manual also contains valuable information for owners who are interested in showing their Westies.

Fascinating color photos will give you an insight into the world of this small dog, which has attained great popularity worldwide.

The author of this book and the editors of Barron's series of nature books wish you a great deal of pleasure with your Westie.

Please read the "Important Notes" on page 63.

West Highland White Terriers: Quick and Self-confident

Nothing escapes this watchful eye. With ears pricked, this Westie is waiting for just the right moment to make a dash.

The Westie, a "Large" Small Dog

With a height of 11 inches (28 cm) at the withers and a weight of about 17 to 22 pounds (8–10 kg), the West Highland white terrier—affectionately known as the Westie—undoubtedly ranks as one of the small breeds of dogs. That, however, is by no means an indication that Westies exhibit the character traits commonly attributed to small dogs. Westies are not delicate or prone to disease; on the contrary, they are robust little animals that like stimulation and exercise, and their training demands the same energy and firmness required with large dogs. The Westie is in no way a lap dog.

A little king. Friendly, even-tempered without being boring, self-confident, courageous, plucky, and quick to learn—these are the typical traits of Westies, the qualities that make them so lovable. The Westie is every inch a king; it greets visitors with serene geniality, does not bark without cause but reports unusual noises, is equally cordial and affectionate with every member of the family, and is always ready to place itself in front of "its" family if danger arises. Although it possesses all the character traits of a guard dog, it is too small in stature to play that role convincingly.

An ideal partner for children. Their equable nature and love of fun make Westies ideal family pets. They love to romp and be in motion, and

they make ideal playmates for children. It is up to the parents, of course, to make it clear to their children that this lovable little dog is not a toy, but an independent creature whose needs and characteristics a child has to respect. Dealing with an animal molds children's character, benefits their development, and sets expectations for them. The dog teaches them without their being aware of it. They learn to act responsibly and independently and to deal appropriately with feelings like aggression or grief.

Some activity and exercise, please! Despite their size, Westies don't like to be carried or to be lugged around in pockets. They want to have all four feet on the ground—and in motion. Their need for exercise is exceptionally great; many Westies easily accompany their master or mistress on a nine-mile (15 km) jog. Because these dogs are alert and quick to learn, they also require attention from you and little tasks to perform in fun (see How-to: Keeping Your Dog Physically Fit, pages 38–39). If your pet lacks this kind of challenge or has no opportunity to let off steam in an appropriate way, it will suffer both intellectually and emotionally.

An apt pupil, but not about to give up hunting. Westies are extremely easy to teach; they catch on quickly and enjoy having tasks to carry out. Nevertheless, like all terriers, they

Its hunting instinct has been aroused. This Westie is digging in the ground.

are stubborn, and during training it is crucial that you be firm in insisting that the dog do exactly what you ask of it. The little animal will quickly find out just who is going to train whom, and if you don't take some precautions, your Westie will do whatever it likes. There is one thing, though, that your Westie, however good a pupil it is, will never be able to unlearn—its passionate love of hunting. That means that the area where your pet is kept has to be securely fenced. Every time you take a walk—even in town—its hunting instinct may be triggered by outward provocations. In this situation, only the leash can keep your pet safe. A dog that is after game is in danger of being inadvertently shot by a hunter or being injured by a motor vehicle.

Other dogs are friends. Westies are not aggressive dogs; their behavior toward others of their kind is friendly and self-assured. They are not inclined to let themselves be intimidated, but react fearlessly and boldly, even where large dogs are concerned. That sometimes can have unpleasant consequences for these little animals.

Appearances that do matter. The Westie's white coat needs a certain amount of grooming to appear neat at all times. Daily brushing is part of the grooming ritual, which may also include being rinsed off with warm water after a walk on muddy paths (see How-to: Grooming, pages 26–27). The Westie has a double coat, consisting of a soft undercoat and a more wiry top coat that is extremely resistant to dirt. As a result of selective breeding, Westies, unlike other dogs, do not shed their hair in spring and fall. Consequently, we have to lend our pets a helping hand and ensure that "molting" takes place, in order to prevent health problems. Westies have to be trimmed about every 12 weeks. That involves thinning and shortening the coat. Your dog's

breeder or your breed club also can teach you to trim a Westie's coat or you can have this task performed by a groomer.

The Origin of the Breed—from a Pack Animal to a Family Pet

The home of the West Highland white terrier is Scotland—more precisely, the mountainous regions in the northern part of the country, the so-called Highlands. Rocky coasts determine the character of the landscape. Large areas of heath crisscrossed by rivers extend over the bleak, rugged terrain. Mountain lakes and high moors alternate, and the climate is harsh and rainy, with stormy winds. The moors, the heath, and the woodlands are inhabited by deer, rabbits, and partridges, which provide an abundance of food for predatory animals. It was the job of the West Highland white terrier and its ancestors to hunt those predators. Hunters needed the help of small, courageous dogs to drive foxes and badgers out of their hard-to-reach dens in the rock.

From dark- to white-coated terriers. English sources tell us that the men who used the dark-coated ancestor of the present-day Westie, the cairn terrier, for hunting in the nineteenth century had an aversion to white dogs and killed the light-colored newborns in each litter. Allegedly they were not equal to the demands of the hunt. One day, however, Colonel Malcolm of Poltalloch had a dreadful hunting accident. He shot his own dark-coated dog, having mistaken it for the game he was pursuing. Deeply grieved, he vowed to raise only white terriers from then on. Unlike the other breeders, he kept the white, or almost-white puppies, in each litter and bred them exclusively, so that over the course of generations he eliminated the dark color from his cairn terrier strain. His dogs, known as Poltalloch

Typical Westie!
This little dog from Scotland was bred for hunting, and as a result its temperament often gets the better of it during a walk. Put your pet on a leash.

terriers or white cairn terriers, soon were held in high esteem. They proved fully as courageous and successful as their dark-coated cousins, and they had an additional advantage—their light color made them easier to distinguish from wildlife, even in darkness and bad weather.

The name West Highland white terrier was adopted at the beginning of the twentieth century. The Scottish Kennel Club officially recognized the breed in October 1904, and recognition from the English Kennel Club followed in 1907.

The Westie as a pet. The first Westies to appear in dog shows in Great Britain in the late nineteenth century were marked by battle scars acquired while hunting. The marks were not held to be a fault, however; on the contrary, they were considered a sign of particular courage and gameness, or suitability for the hunt. Although the Westie continued to be prized as a hunting dog, over time it became more important in the role of friendly household companion. Westies were exhibited with growing frequency at dog shows, and in the course of time their outward appearance was altered by selective breeding. The dog became more compact; its back was shorter, its coat, thicker. Such a coat tends to be a drawback in a hunting dog, but in a show animal more emphasis is placed on appearance, and the thick coat became highly desirable. Today the coat remains a typical feature of the Westie's outward appearance. Westies now are kept predominantly as family pets; only in extremely rare cases are they still employed as hunters. They still retain their hunting instincts, however, and no Westie owner should underestimate their fighting spirit. Not only is the terrier's hunting instinct still intact—with the result that the dog takes off as soon as it picks up a scent—but the Westie is also, so to speak, a "hunting dog out of work." In order to be content, it needs to be stimulated and kept busy. Many of our dogs' behavioral problems today can be traced to the fact that they do not have enough to keep them busy. For owners, that means spending plenty of time with their Westie, giving it tasks that will be fun, and—not least of all—making sure the dog can stay active and let off steam.

Black and white together: A West Highland white-terrier and a Scottish terrier.

These two dogs—a Westie and a Scottish terrier—are tussling wildly over their toy, an old shoe. For a dog that enjoys being in motion as much as the West Highland white terrier, it is crucial to have a chance to really let off steam once a day.

The Breed Standard

The breed standard is a description of the ideal type of a breed. It is drawn up in the country of origin, deposited with the International Federation of Dog Breeders (an umbrella organization), and distributed to the individual member organizations, so that they have uniform criteria for assessing each dog breed.

General appearance: The Westie is a small, robust terrier with no small amount of self-esteem. It is strongly

A Westie that conforms to the breed standard.

built, deep in chest and back ribs, with straight back, powerful hindquarters, and muscular legs.

Temperament: Happy, alert, courageous, self-reliant, friendly.

Movement: Free, straight, with strong drive from the powerful muscles of the hindquarters. Faults are stiff or stilty movement behind and cowhocks (a certain defect in stance; see drawing, page 11).

Skull: The skull should be slightly domed, the head densely covered with hair. It must be carried at no more than a 90° angle to the neck axis and must never be thrust forward. The length of the head from the occipital bone to the eyes should only slightly exceed the distance from the eyes to the nose.

Nose: Black and fairly large. It must not protrude and give the face a pointed look.

Eyes: Medium in size, widely set apart, and as dark in color as possible. They look out sharply and intelligently from under heavy eyebrows. Light-colored eyes are objectionable.

Ears: Small, erect, terminating in a sharp point, and carried self-confidently. They are set neither too far apart nor too closely together.

Teeth: Because of the mandatory jaunty look, the bite should be as wide set as necessary between the two canine teeth. There shall be six incisor teeth between the canines of both upper and lower jaws. The teeth should be set perpendicular to the jaw and should be large, relative to the overall size of the dog. A tight scissors bite is required, with the upper incisors slightly overlapping the lower incisors without any gap. An edge-to-edge bite (level mouth) is equally acceptable.

Neck: It must be long enough to make the requisite head position possible. It is muscular, becoming broader toward the base and merging into nicely sloping shoulders.

Shoulders: Laid back at an angle, with broad shoulder blades that lie close to the chest. The joint between the shoulder blade and the foreleg should be set well forward, with the elbows close to permit free movement.

Front legs: Short, straight, muscular, thickly covered with short hard hair.

Body: Compact, level back, loins broad and strong.

Hindquarters: Powerful, muscular, and broad in the upper part. The legs are short, muscular, and sinewy. The thighs should be very muscular and not set wide apart. The hocks are well bent and drawn close under the body.

Whether standing still or moving, the hind legs are fairly close together.

Feet: The forefeet are larger than the hind ones, they are covered with short bristly hair, and they are round, strong, and thickly padded. The hind feet are also thickly padded. The bottom of the pads and all the nails should most desirably be black in color.

Tail: Never docked; 5 to 6 inches (13–15 cm) long, covered with wiry hair, and as straight as possible. It should not be curled over the back and should be set on high enough so that the spine does not appear to slope down to it.

Coat: The outer coat consists of straight firm hair about 2 inches (5–6 cm) long. The undercoat is furlike, short, soft, and thick.

Color: Pure white.

Height at withers: About 11 inches (28 cm).

Note: Males should have two normally developed testicles, completely descended in the scrotum.

Brief Profile of the Westie

Breed: West Highland white terrier.

Group: Terriers.

Size and weight: Height at the withers about 11 inches (28 cm), weight between about 17 and 22 pounds (8–10 kg).

Character and general appearance: Small, robust, self-confident dog. Strongly built, with level back and muscular legs. Cheerful, friendly household companion, alert, not a barker.

Suitable for: People who have plenty of time to spend with their dog. Good family pet, good with children.

Not suitable for: People who view this handsome dog as a fashionable accessory and want to treat it as a lap dog.

Diseases typical of the breed: Craniomandibular osteopathy (CMO; see page 45). Itching and allergic skin inflammations, often caused by improper grooming and poor nutrition.

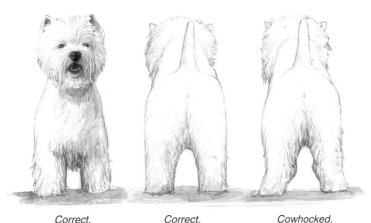

Even the stance of the forelegs and hind legs is precisely defined in the description of the breed standard.

Correct.   Correct.   Cowhocked.

When a Westie Joins Your Household

With this look in its eyes, the Westie will capture your heart. When buying a dog, also keep in mind the needs of the animal which you will have to fulfill.

Will a Westie Fit Into Your Life?

Spontaneity is a fine thing, but completely misplaced when it comes to acquiring a dog. Buying a Westie just on a whim is an egotistical, irresponsible act. A dog that joins your household is a new member of the family, a creature that can live 15 years or more, with needs that its owner is responsible for satisfying. For these reasons, before buying such an animal you need to think very carefully about whether a Westie is right for you. Consider these points:

• Can you devote enough time to your Westie? Dogs are pack animals, and intensive contact with humans is essential to their psychological development. A Westie that is left alone for more than four hours each day will suffer; it will lack incentive, and its faculties will become dulled. Your mere presence is not enough, however; you also have to show your Westie a great deal of attention. It has to be groomed and fed, and it needs several fairly long walks every day.

• A Westie is not inexpensive. In addition to the purchase price—a Westie from a reputable breeder costs from $250 to approximately $1200 for a show-quality animal—there are the day-to-day expenses to consider: food, grooming (your Westie has to go to the "hairdresser" every 10 to 12 weeks), veterinary fees, dog license fees.

• What will become of the dog if for example, you get sick, or have to visit a health facility—a hospital or retirement home? If you are single, what will happen if you meet someone who doesn't like your Westie? Who will take care of the dog when you go on vacation (see page 30)?

• Will your landlord allow you to keep a dog?

• Is any member of your family allergic to dog hair? If you are unsure, consult your doctor before buying a dog.

• Are all the members of your family in agreement about the purchase of a Westie? Don't present the dog as a surprise gift—its acquisition needs to be discussed in the family and supported by everyone. Children need to be ready to learn that the Westie is a play*mate*, but definitely not a play*thing*.

• Is a Westie the right dog for you? Westies are buoyant, active dogs that need a great deal of exercise. Older people in particular often find Westies too much for them to handle, and they should ask themselves whether a different dog breed might be more appropriate to their needs.

A Male or a Female?

I have never noticed any gender-related differences in the temperaments of my Westies. Males and females (bitches) are equally lively, courageous, affectionate, and devoted. Nevertheless, I recommend that first-time dog owners buy a female, because she will be easier to train. That does not mean, however, that you need to be any less firm with her—although she will disobey commands less readily than a male.

Don't worry: When dogs are playing, the fight often looks rougher than it is.

Unspayed bitches come into heat twice a year (see page 51).

A Puppy or a Full-grown Dog?

Raising a puppy and watching as it develops is a wonderful task. The little animal becomes a part of the family and is molded by it in turn; a close bond is forged. On the other hand, of course, you have to invest a great deal of time and effort to housebreak the dog and train it properly. If you adopt an adult animal, you can avoid all that work. However, you will need to supply plenty of patience and understanding, because changing owners involves a huge readjustment for any dog. If you let the dog know that you are fond of it, the typical Westie will soon adapt to its new family and settle down well.

One Westie or Two?

What is nicer than one Westie? Two Westies! For the dog, it is enjoyable to have another of its kind join the "family pack." Apart from the daily grooming session, you don't need any more time for two dogs than for one. In fact, the opposite is true. Your time is less in demand, because the dogs generally keep each other occupied. All the expenses are doubled, however, and if you take a vacation or get sick, it is harder to find temporary accommodations for two dogs than for one.

If you don't want to have one of the dogs castrated, it makes more sense to keep dogs of the same sex and get them used to each other while still young. If you keep a male and a bitch together, problems arise during estrus. If you already have an adult Westie that has been in residence for some time, a puppy is the only dog you will be able to add. Your full-grown Westie will not put up with another mature dog of the same sex in its territory. Make sure that the first dog retains its previous rights, and show it preferential treatment at the beginning, to keep your older pet from feeling dethroned.

Westies and Other Pets

The Westie's friendly temperament enables it to fit easily into an existing pack. My Westies, for example, live in harmony with six cats, an Irish wolfhound, and an Old English sheepdog. Admittedly, I am never allowed to forget that Westies are hunting dogs; although my Westies do accept my cats, they will hunt any others. Caution is called for, however, if you have small animals such as parakeets, hamsters, rabbits, or guinea pigs, which cannot defend themselves against a Westie. Never leave those animals and a Westie together without supervision.

Westie Buyers: Caveat Emptor!

Unfortunately, the West Highland white terrier has suffered the worst fate that can possibly befall a dog breed—it has become trendy. As a result, the price of puppies has climbed sky high, which in turn has

Typical Westie!

If danger threatens, this dog will courageously step out in front of "its" family, but it is too small to be taken seriously as a protector— so don't make demands of that kind on your Westie.

Choosing Your Puppy

• A healthy puppy is typically lively, bright, and inquisitive. It should rush up to the breeder, not remain sitting shyly in a corner.
• Puppies with smooth hair should be given preference, because they later will have the desirable wiry coat.
• Have the breeder show you the puppy's teeth. A responsible breeder, without being asked, will make you aware of any malocclusion and offer you a reduction in price.
• A distended abdomen is a symptom of worm infestation and thus an indication that the breeder has not wormed the puppies adequately.
• In a male, both testicles should be palpable. Don't exert hard pressure on them. Let the breeder help you check them.

induced irresponsible "breeders" to produce more puppies. In choosing animals for mating, they have ceased to ensure that both parents have the typical Westie temperament, are in good health, and are free from anatomical faults. That much is obvious in the puppies that result from such unions; at best they still can only be described as "Westie-like." For this reason, it is crucial to proceed with a critical eye when choosing a breeder.

How to Find a Good Breeder

• To get a Westie that conforms to the breed standard, is in good health, and also possesses the lovable, typical temperament of this breed, your best bet is to consult the West Highland White Terrier Club of America (WHWTCA) or the American Kennel Club (AKC; for addresses, see page

63). Both organizations have codes of ethics which the breeders are expected to follow. The AKC does on occasion inspect the records and facilities of a breeder, which usually occurs after a complaint or if the breeder has a high volume of litters.

I can only warn you not to buy a dog from any of the "Westie producers" (I hesitate to call them breeders) who are not registered with respectable clubs and whose only goal is to produce more and more litters. Although they will certainly provide you with a pedigree, it will lack official recognition.
• Visit several breeders and check carefully to see whether the breeder lives for his or her dogs or just lives off them. Good breeders have close contact with the dogs. Both the mother dog and the little puppies are relaxed and show no fear in their behavior toward the breeder. Insist that you also see the mother dog, and make sure that the animals are kept clean and well groomed, as these factors are fundamental to the puppies' good health. You will have to accept, however, that for reasons of hygiene many breeders do not allow buyers to enter the breeding room.

Caution: Under no circumstances should you buy a Westie from "puppy mills." They offer several breeds for sale. Even though the dog trade has puppies available more cheaply than a recognized breeder, your money will be poorly invested, because in all likelihood the animal will become ill and be emotionally unstable.

If you do buy an animal from a puppy mill-supplied pet shop—even if it is only out of pity—you are lending support to the misery of the brood bitches that are forced to produce puppies for this trade. Often they are mated when only six months old and then forced to bear a litter after every heat, without a break, until their bodies can no longer do so. Not infrequently, they are simply put to death at that point.

Vaccination Certificate, Worming, and Feeding Schedule

When the puppies are eight to nine weeks old, they are ready to go to their new homes. At this time the Westie also gets its first inoculation (see Vaccination Schedule, page 43), which is recorded on the Certificate of Vaccination. The breeder will give you that document when you buy the dog. Make sure that it is completely filled out. Before the dog is handed over, you also need to ask whether it has been wormed (see page 43).

A Westie has to be brushed every day to keep its coat looking well-groomed at all times.

If a treat is in the offing, your Westie is more than willing to sit up and beg for it.

Responsible breeders give the buyer a feeding schedule, because it is important for the puppy to continue getting its accustomed foods. A sudden switch to a different diet can result in stomach and intestinal upsets.

The Pedigree

The pedigree is a record or document in the legal sense; the buyer whose name appears there is the legal owner of the dog. The document is the property of the breeders association and must be returned to that organization after the death of the Westie.

Basically, anyone who wants to be a breeder in the United States can be one. Whether they are a reputable breeder or not is another matter. A sire and dam of a litter should be registered with the American Kennel Club in order for the puppies to be registerable, and every dog should have an AKC registration number. These entries are particularly important if you want to breed or show your Westie. Even if you have no such plans, you should attach great importance to the recognized pedigree, because by buying a dog from a supervised breeder you are helping to put a stop to the unscrupulous large-scale breeding of the dog trade, and thus supporting the prevention of cruelty to animals.

The Contract of Sale

When you purchase a Westie, insist on having a bill of sale. It provides legal safeguards for both the buyer and the breeder. Under law, the purchase of a dog is a civil matter. The bill of sale is helpful if legal disputes arise.

Basic Equipment and Accessories for Your Westie

Dog basket: Westies prefer a sleeping place that resembles a cave, offering protection on all sides. The bed has to be large enough to let the dog stretch out comfortably. A large, enclosed or cavelike cat basket is suitable (make sure the dog doesn't bite the wickerwork and injure itself), or a carrier made of plastic or fiberglass. The dog will sleep with the carrier door open, of course. You can take the basket or the carrier along on trips, and the dog will be able to feel at home everywhere. A blanket, thick towel, or a pad (available in pet stores) can serve as bedding.

Collar and leash: To get the puppy used to walking on a leash, the best solution is a so-called show lead, which is available in pet stores. A leash and a collar all in one, it is made of light, tear-resistant nylon cord that does not weigh too heavily on a puppy. Later, once the Westie is running along on its leash at your side, other styles will be appropriate: a leather collar and leather leash for walks in town, and a leash that retracts automatically (with about 16 feet [5 m] of play) for walks in fields or woods. Harnesses are uncomfortable for Westies and damage their hair.

Food and water dishes: Dishes or bowls made of stainless steel are advisable, because they can be washed hygienically in boiling-hot water and cannot be gnawed by your puppy. The dishes should always stand in the same spot, because your dog needs to have drinking water available round the clock. Look for a food dish with a rubber ring underneath to prevent it from sliding around the room when the dog eats. Be sure to obtain a feeding dish that is large (or small) enough for your pet.

Last but not least, it is a good idea to keep an automatic waterer always available to ensure that it never goes thirsty.

Toys: Don't forget to provide some toys. They are very important for young dogs, which want—and need—to use

Healthy puppies are bright and inquisitive. The task of training them and watching them develop is a delightful one.

their teeth. A great variety of products is available in stores, but by no means are all of them completely safe for dogs. Many toys include those made of rawhide, which will let your puppy satisfy its need to chew.

Although rawhide toys are popular and have been used for many years, there are experts who do not recommend them because there have been cases of dogs who managed to tear out rawhide particles which then became stuck in their throats. An alternative is the artificial bone, such a Nylabone® or Gumabone® (the latter is for softer teeth), which comes in different sizes and is artificially flavored.

The problem is that puppies and young dogs need something strong enough to chew on while their teeth and jaws are developing. They need it to cut their puppy teeth, to promote the growth of permanent teeth, to help remove the puppy teeth later on, and to set the permanent teeth in the jaws. What is best? Rawhide, a natural product that has been the delight of generations of pets but one that presents some degree of danger, or a totally safe but totally artificial product? The decision is yours.

Any balls and rings should be small enough for the Westie to hold in its mouth—but too large for it to swallow (see How-to: Keeping Your Dog Physically Fit, page 38).

Toys made of thin plastic or any material that splinters easily are unsuitable. Many of the squeaking toys available in stores are dangerous, because your Westie can choke on parts of the plastic covering or on the noise-maker itself.

Grooming accessories: For grooming your Westie (see How-to: Grooming, pages 26–27), you need a currying brush for terriers and a wire brush with rubberized cushion beneath. These products are sold in pet stores. If you decide to trim your pet yourself, you will also need thinning shears, regular scissors, and a heavy-duty, blunt trimming knife.

Dog food: Before the puppy joins your household, ask the breeder what dog food you should buy. If necessary, have the breeder give you some of the puppy's usual food—switching to a different diet always entails some problems.

To reach their goal, they'll dig a tunnel in the ground if necessary.

Hazards in Your Home

Source of Danger	Possible Effects	How to Avoid
Balcony	Westie may fall	Install safeguard (nets available in pet stores)
Chemicals, detergents, cleansers	Poisoning, acid burns if licked up	Store in tightly closed cupboards; don't use any chemical weed-killers or pesticides in the yard
Plants	Poisoning, injury	Put poisonous or thorny plants out of dog's reach, or don't keep such plants at all
Electric wires, wall sockets	Electrocution	Run wires behind walls; don't leave exposed cords plugged in when not in use; cover wall sockets with childproof covers (available where electrical appliances are sold)
Broken fragments, nails, needles	Cuts in paw area; dog can swallow the foreign objects	Don't leave dangerous objects lying around
Steep, overhanging, or open stairs	Fall, brain concussion, skull fracture, broken legs	Block access with child safety gate (commercially available); carry the dog on stairs
Pond, swimming pool	Drowning	Prevent access by surrounding with fence; install climbing aids
Yard	Running away	Fence in the yard (fence height about 4 feet 3 inches [1.30 m]; must be impossible to dig under; Westies can slip through latticework fences and hedges)
Doors	Being caught and squashed in door, being locked out or in	Watch out when closing door; avoid drafts
Children's toys	Swallowing foreign objects	Don't leave small toys (like Lego pieces or marbles) lying around

Acclimation and the Westie's Daily Routine

The time has come. The puppy is eight or nine weeks old and ready for you to pick it up at the breeder's. This is the beginning of a wonderful, exciting period, in which, however, you have to adapt your own daily routine to accommodate the new family member.

After doing its typical excavation work, your Westie may come home looking like this, with a mud-smeared muzzle.

Bringing Your New Puppy Home in the Car

You will need a second person with you when you bring the puppy home in the car from the breeder's. Your companion can hold the squirming little Westie on his or her lap during the trip. Make sure that the puppy is not exposed to any drafts; it is sensitive to drafty air. Take along an old towel as the little animal may throw up out of excitement or from motion sickness.

If you use public transportation, put the puppy in a carrier (available in pet stores) that can be latched securely.

If your Westie is to be the second dog in your household, it is a good idea to bring along your other dog when you pick up the new puppy, so that the two have their first meeting at the breeder's—on neutral ground.

Pick up the dog early in the day. It will then have time to explore its new home thoroughly before it has to sleep alone for the first time that evening—without its mother or brothers and sisters.

Tip: Several days before the scheduled pick-up, give the breeder the blanket on which your dog will be sleeping and ask him or her to put it in the puppy room. By the time the dog changes owners, the blanket will have acquired a familiar smell, which will make it easier for the little animal to get used to its new home.

The First Few Days at Home

Once in your home, the puppy will sniff everything curiously and investigate its new surroundings. Let it do so undisturbed.

Stress-free acclimation. The first few days, avoid all hustle and bustle; let the little dog have a chance to develop trust in its new family.

Under no circumstances should you give a party to celebrate the puppy's arrival. Don't let your friends and neighbors see your new housemate until it has had a chance to adjust.

How to pick up the puppy. If you want to pick up the puppy, you need to talk to it first. To lift it, place one hand under the little dog's chest, the other beneath its hindquarters. Never lift the puppy by the nape or by the forelegs; that could cause it pain.

The puppy's own special place. The very first day, assign the dog a special place of its own. Once the Westie has chosen its favorite spot, you can put down a blanket there for it. Westies are inquisitive, and they prefer a place from which they can share in whatever is going on around them. A cold floor and drafty air—even drafts under the doors—are bad for the dog. At night, a room temperature of about 65°F (18°C) is ideal. If you don't want the dog to share the sofa or armchair with you, you have to forbid it to do so from the very start.

West Highland white terriers make ideal playmates for children.

HOW-TO:
Training

Start training your Westie as soon as the puppy comes to live in your home. The so-called socialization phase begins in the ninth week of life, and dogs are most willing to learn during this time. Take advantage of

1. Walking on a leash is one of the most important exercises.

this phase, but when training your pet, keep in mind that a dog can connect praise or criticism only with the action that immediately precedes it. And don't forget—the most important ingredient of your Westie's training is firmness.

The major training objective is housebreaking the puppy (see page 24). Additional training goals that you need to set include the following:

Leash Breaking
Drawing 1

No puppy enjoys having the collar and leash put on it for the first time. For that reason, you need to arm yourself with patience when you practice "walking on the leash." Do the exercise several times a day, limiting each session to 10 or 15 minutes at first.

Putting on the collar. Put the collar of the show lead (available in pet stores) on the Westie, leaving room for one of your fingers to fit between the collar and your pet's neck and making sure that the dog can't slip its head out. Attach the end of the lead to a 16-foot (5 m) leash that retracts automatically.

Letting the dog run and shortening the leash. Let the Westie run on the long leash, and shorten it from time to time. If the dog responds by stopping and balking, don't pull on the leash, and never drag the puppy along behind you. Instead, stay where you are and coax the dog to come to you. Be patient—it may take five minutes for the Westie to come. Once it pats toward you, praise it. Then let it run a little more on the long leash. In each phase of the exercise, repeat this several times, gradually increasing the period of time the dog runs on the shortened leash.

The Command "Sit"
Drawing 2

As you utter the command "Sit," gently press the dog's hindquarters downward with your palm. Praise the Westie, even if it stays seated only a short time. Take your time with this exercise, and don't ask too

2. "Sit": With your palm, carefully press the dog's hindquarters downward.

much of the dog. The Westie need not master it in a week.

The Command "Phooey"
Drawing 3

This command is intended to show the Westie that some things are off limits to it. Here, too, you need to be firm in making it clear just what your pet is

3. "Phooey," if uttered in a stern voice, tells the Westie to refrain from doing something.

allowed to do and what is taboo. Every undesirable behavior should be followed immediately with a stern "Phooey."

The Command "Come"

Squat down on the floor and coax the little puppy to come to you, using the same command each time: "Come" or "Come here." If it runs to you, praise it. Even if it takes a long time for the dog to obey your command, don't fuss at it when it finally comes. All the puppy would learn is this lesson: I get scolded when I come.

During the puppy stage, you should carefully consider whether it makes sense to call the little animal just when its attention is claimed by something interesting. Often it is better to wait until its interest level has dropped and then call it. By waiting, you will avoid having the dog "miss" your command, which you can't let it get away with later on.

If the Westie totally refuses to come when called, you need to punish it right at the spot where it ignores the command. You can throw a leash or a light chain at the dog. Your ability to show your displeasure from a distance will make a big impression, and in future the Westie will be quicker to obey.

The Exercise "Staying Alone"

Once the Westie is familiar with its new surroundings, you can gradually get it used to staying alone. Put the dog in a room where there are no sources of danger. Give your pet its toys and some rawhide objects to chew (see drawing, page 39) to keep it from becoming bored. Give the command "Wait" or "Stay," and leave the room. Don't wait quietly outside the door. The puppy will know that you are there, whimper, and want to come to you. Leave the house or apartment. When you come back, praise the Westie, and be sure to reward it with a "treat" for staying alone.

Basic Rules of Dog Training

Drawing 4

Firmness is essential. Training a Westie requires patience, persistence, time, and, above all, firmness. It has to be clear from the outset what the dog may and may not do, and all the members of the family have to enforce the same rules. Everyone in the family needs to agree to use the same words when giving the dog commands or praising and scolding it. Don't forget—your Westie is extremely stubborn. Once it has succeeded in getting its way, it will try to do so repeatedly. That is why you can't let bad behavior, such as begging for food at the table, even begin.

Dogs are pack animals. The pack adheres to fixed rules that give each individual dog a sense of safety and security, because each one has its own place in the hierarchy. Only the leader of the pack decides what the group will do. For this reason, a dog expects its human pack leader to lay down completely unambiguous rules. The Westie needs to know what is permanently forbidden and what behavior is expected of it. Antiauthoritarian methods of training are inappropriate for dogs, which learn from experience and want to repeat pleasant things as often as possible, while avoiding unpleasant ones.

Hitting is not a training aid. The Westie will only become timid and fearful and mistrust you. Instead, praise your pet for good behavior and punish bad behavior with loud scolding. One suitable way to punish a dog is to pick it up briefly by the nape and shake it.

4. Begging for food at the table is taboo. The Westie should lie obediently under your chair.

The Westie's submissive attitude means: "I'm giving up. Please don't hurt me."

The First Few Nights

Although the puppy has been distracted by all the new impressions in the daytime, at night it will realize that it is separated from its mother and siblings. I recommend to the people who buy puppies from me that they not let the dog sleep alone the first few nights. Put a box or an enclosed basket (see drawing, page 30) in your bedroom. Another alternative is to sleep in the room where you want the dog to sleep in future. The puppy will hear you breathing and, no longer feeling alone, will sleep contentedly. You need to have the Westie under your supervision at night anyway, because it has to be housebroken. Locking the puppy in a room by itself is cruel. It has never been alone in its life, and it will express its misery loudly, keeping the entire family awake.

If you let the dog into your bed the first night, you have to be prepared to do so for the rest of its life. A dog does not understand why it is allowed in your bed one day, but not the next.

Housebreaking

The first lesson the puppy has to learn is not to relieve itself inside your house. On pages 22 and 23 you learned how to teach your Westie the other things it needs to know to live with your family.

A puppy has an inborn reluctance to soil its own bed. Putting this instinct to our own use, we train the puppy to be housebroken. It can take three or four weeks to achieve this goal. During this time you need to pay a great deal of attention to the puppy—keep a close eye on it and ascertain its cycle for relieving itself. The more closely you watch the dog during the "damp

This mother and her puppy are intently watching the actions of the other dogs.

phase" of its life, the fewer mishaps there will be.

Take it out regularly. A puppy cannot hold its urine for hours at a time. That applies to the nighttime as well. You need to take your pet outdoors after every meal and every nap, so that it can relieve itself there. Praise the dog afterward.

How the puppy makes its needs known. A little Westie produces a puddle very quickly, and it will do so without giving you any advance notice. If it has to defecate, it will first move faster and faster, its nose to the ground, then turn around in a circle, arch its back, and press down. You have to intervene before it arches its back. Carry the dog outside. Praise it once it has done its business.

If an accident happens. If you catch the puppy relieving itself indoors, scold it and take it out right away. A dog can make a connection only if the praise or scolding immediately follows the action. If you discover its "misbehavior" later, it is useless to scold the dog. Clean the spot with disinfectant or with a vinegar and water solution to remove the odor, as the puppy will tend to use the same place again if it smells of urine.

Feed your puppy at set times, then it will also "do its business" at fixed times. This regularity, in turn, will accelerate the process of housebreaking.

Typical Westie!
A Westie quickly learns who will give in to its stubbornness. The only solution is firm training.

HOW-TO:
Grooming

Grooming your Westie not only keeps the dog looking attractive and assures you of a clean housemate, but also contributes to the animal's well-being and continued good health (see Drawing 4).

1. You can pluck the top coat with your fingers.

Grooming the Coat
Drawings 1 and 2

Maintaining the coat. For daily brushing, set the Westie on a table that has a skidproof top (rubber mat; see drawing, page 15). With one hand, hold the puppy still to keep it from jumping off the table; with the other, brush it with a currying brush for terriers. If your pet is full-grown, brush it first with the terrier brush, then with a wire brush to keep the hair from becoming matted.

Showers instead of baths. Bathing the dog with soap or shampoo removes the natural

26

oils in its coat that protect the animal from wet and cold. Illness can be the result. Your Westie will always be perfectly well groomed if you brush it daily, rinse the hair on the dog's legs and its ears, if necessary, with warm water, and give it a warm shower once a week, making sure that no water gets into its ears (put cotton in them). Keep the Westie out of drafts while its coat is wet. If your dog has rolled in something malodorous, use a moisturizing shampoo for pets or baby shampoo and wash only the affected areas of its coat.

Trimming. The Westie has a double coat, consisting of a wiry, rough top coat and a soft undercoat. The top coat protects the dog from cold and damp; the undercoat keeps it warm. If you simply cut off the top coat, it will take about a year for the Westie's protective hair to grow back. Instead, the coat has to be trimmed, that is, plucked. You can do that either with your fingers or with a dull

2. A dull trimming knife is an ideal tool for use in the trimming process.

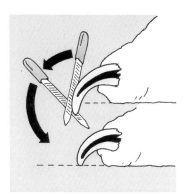

3. Using a nail file, file the tip of the nail back to the imaginary line.

trimming knife. The knife is useful in the trimming process because it covers a larger surface area. Have your Westie properly trimmed by a professional every three months. If you want to trim your pet yourself, learn only from a professional.

Trimming the Nails
Drawing 3

A dog that moves about a great deal on a hard abrasive surface keeps its own nails worn down. The nails have to be trimmed if the tip of the nail extends beyond an imaginary line reaching from the foot pad to the nail. A portion of the nail is furnished with blood vessels and nerves. For laymen it is hard to tell where it is safe to cut without injury to the dog. Each time, remove only a tiny piece of the curved nail tip with your clippers. It is preferable to use a special nail file for dogs (available in pet stores) or an emery board. File the nails to the right length.

Foot Care

The hairs between the foot pads protect the feet from injury. Trim only the surplus hair that protrudes. Once a week, feel between the pads with a finger, and cut out only the hard clumps of hair stuck together with dirt. In winter, rub the Westie's feet with Vaseline for protection.

Teeth

Inspect your Westie's teeth every three months; check for tartar, which is visible as a hardened, brownish deposit at the neck of the tooth. Tartar formation is the result of eating overly soft foods. For this reason, once a week give the Westie a small soup bone (beef) that has been boiled first. Boiled oxtails are perfect for this. If the gums are inflamed, if you discover a loose or broken tooth, or if the dog drools excessively or has foul breath, you need to take it to the veterinarian.

Ears

Drawing 5

The ear is a sensitive organ that should be left undisturbed as far as possible. Approximately every three months, use tweezers to pluck any hairs growing out of the ear, in order to keep the auditory canal clear. Pluck out only a few hairs each time, to keep from hurting the dog. These hairs must not be cut, because tiny pieces of hair would drop into the ear. If necessary, you can clean the outer part of the ear with a cotton swab soaked with baby oil.

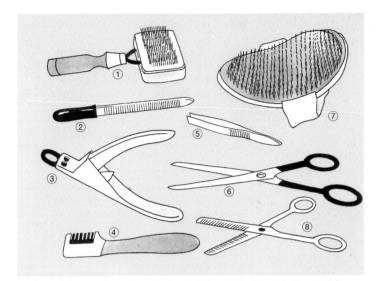

4. Essential grooming aids: wire brush (1), nail file (2), nail clippers (3), trimming knife (4), tweezers (5), scissors (6), plucking brush (7), thinning shears (8).

Eyes

If mucoid matter has collected in the corners of your pet's eyes, remove it with a cloth handkerchief. If the matter has become encrusted, moisten the cloth with a camomile solution

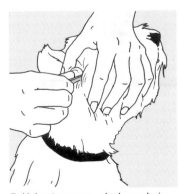

5. Using tweezers, pluck any hairs that grow out of the ear.

and carefully loosen the crust with it.

If the Westie has weeping eyes, the cause frequently is hair that sticks out horizontally from the end of the nose and grows right into the eyes. This irritation can lead to conjunctivitis. Always cut the hair short (without injuring the eye), or lubricate the hair with Vaseline and keep smoothing it away from the eye until it grows long enough not to cause trouble.

Westies' Behavior

Like all members of its species, the Westie has retained some behavioral patterns that have their roots deep in the ancestral past, among the wolves. Every dog, for example, has an innate mastery of the common language that governs dogs' dealings with each other. We divide it into articulate language and body language.

Articulate Language

The sounds presented here are only elements of the basic language; each Westie has its own broad range of vocal expression. Learn to listen and to respond in your own way. That is part of the intimate relationship you can build with your dog.

Barking. During the process of domestication, dogs learned to bark. Your Westie uses barking as a means of warning you. Barking can also be an expression of joy or an invitation to play.

Growling. This sound is a threat. If it is meant seriously, the hairs on the dog's nape will stand up and the animal will bare its teeth. A Westie also reacts by growling when it hears something threatening.

Yelping. This is a sign of fear or pain. A puppy employs this sound calculatedly, if it is being attacked too roughly in play, for example, and has no chance to defend itself.

Whimpering. This sound could be translated as "Please." Please come for a walk with me. Please feed me. But also—Please help me, I hurt.

Howling. A primitive sound that clearly points to the dog's descent from the wolf. By howling, an animal of that species that had become separated from the pack called attention to itself. It signifies loneliness.

Body Language

To convey their feelings, Westies use body language far more often than sounds. The same rule applies here: Watch your pet closely and become familiar with its own individual mode of expression.

Giving you its paw. This action has its origin in "milking"—the pressing movements of the puppy's paws as it sucks at its mother's teats. All dogs can do this. If your Westie touches you with its paw, it is trying to calm you or asking you to play or go for a walk.

Pushing at you with its nose. This is the Westie's way of emphatically calling your attention to something. If it wants to be patted, it nudges you with its nose; if you don't react, it will push its entire head under your hand.

Licking your face. Granted, not all of us like having a dog's wet tongue in our face. This gesture, however, is the Westie's way of showing that it loves you and acknowledges you as a higher-ranking member of its own kind. Your pet will push its nose against the corner of your mouth, then lick with its tongue. That is the way puppies greet their mother and beg to be fed. Turn your head away if this behavior bothers you, then say a few affectionate words to the dog, but don't scold it.

Lying down on its back. In a conflict with other dogs, the one that displays its unprotected belly is giving a signal that it is defeated. The stronger dog then stops fighting the underdog. In dealing with you, the dog uses this gesture to indicate that it feels safe or that it is subjugating itself to you.

Ear signals. A dog's ears and tail are the most important barometers for its mood. Because a Westie's ears and tail are not docked, it can convey the state of its feelings clearly. Typical for the Westie are erect, "pricked" ears, which indicate self-confidence and attentiveness. Laid-back ears mean lack of confidence or even aggression, if the dog also growls or bares its teeth.

Tail signals. Wagging is a sign of joyous excitement; the happier your

Typical Westie!

This dog is very active and wants to be kept busy; you need to allot plenty of time to spend with it. Play with your dog, and get fit—and stay fit— yourself.

Westie is, the more vigorously it wags its tail. A loosely carried tail is an expression of relaxation or contentment. A tail pointing straight up in the air is a sign of extreme excitement and alertness, while a tail that is tucked denotes fear and uncertainty.

Marking and sniffing. When the male raises his leg, he is marking his territory with urine. For this purpose, he chooses prominent features such as tree trunks, posts, or corners of houses. The next male that passes by makes his territorial claims known by covering the first mark. Extremely self-assured male Westies will get up on their front legs for that purpose, doing a kind of handstand to make their mark as high as possible and to seem taller than they really are. Bitches generally do not mark. On occasion, an exceptionally self-confident female will place her own mark over that of a male. If the bitch is in heat, she releases urine as a scent mark, to attract males. Let your Westie sniff to its heart's content when you are out for a walk, so that it doesn't miss any scent marks. This is the dog's way of collecting information about its environment and conveying information about itself. Marking and sniffing are as important for dogs as writing and reading letters are for us.

Vacationing with or without Your Westie?

Before every vacation this question arises: Is the dog coming along or staying behind? The answer certainly depends on your destination: If you're going on vacation to Europe, it's all right for the dog to go along. A few European countries, however—including England, Ireland, Norway, and Sweden—have strict quarantine regulations that make it impossible to take the dog with you. In the United States a similar quarantine is in effect for Hawaii. If you are planning a trip to

Males in particular mark their territory by urinating.

After depositing its stool, the dog scrapes the ground vigorously.

This attitude is meant to encourage you to play.

29

some far-away spot or a tour of large cities exclusively, with the emphasis on seeing places of cultural interest, you should ask yourself whether it might not be better to leave the dog with friends, relatives, neighbors, or, if necessary, a kennel that boards animals.

Traveling by car. Your Westie will enjoy riding in a car. Like a child, it belongs in the back seat, where it needs to be restrained by some kind of safety harness. Pet stores offer sev-

Westies feel at ease in a cavelike basket (available in pet stores).

eral types of products for that purpose. A Westie is much too inquisitive to remain lying down on the floor in front of the passenger seat. In addition, your plans ought to include stopping regularly for a break, to let your pet stretch its legs.

Traveling by train. You will have to buy the dog its own ticket (child's fare), and you may have your Westie in the compartment with you, if your fellow passengers have no objection.

Traveling by plane. The Westie usually is required to travel in a carrier in the cargo compartment, because it often exceeds the weight limit for dogs traveling in the passenger cabin. Be aware that the experience of riding in the cargo hold may possibly be unsettling for the little animal.

If the dog stays behind. If none of your friends or acquaintances can take care of your dog while you are away, you can place an ad in the classified section of the newspaper, under the heading "Livestock, Pets, & Poultry," and try to find a place to board the dog in that way. You also can make a reciprocal arrangement with another dog owner to take care of each other's pets during vacation. If the dogs involved are of the same sex, however, problems may result if the host (or hostess) dog defends its territory.

If you put your pet in a boarding kennel, it is essential to inspect it first. Compare several such establishments, talk to the managers, and look at the dogs. Make sure that they are well groomed and seem alert and happy. Generally speaking, putting the dog in a boarding kennel ought to be your last choice, because your pet will suffer greatly from the unaccustomed experience of being caged. It will assume that it is being deprived permanently of its loved ones and its familiar routines. There is no way to make a dog understand that it will be picked up again after your trip.

The Aging Westie

With proper nutrition and grooming and appropriate living conditions, a Westie easily can live to an age of 15 years or more. From a purely external standpoint, your pet will not look its age; it won't get any gray hairs. With my older Westies, I often didn't notice any age-related changes in their behavior until they were over 10 years old. Their naps and rest breaks start to get

Checklist: Taking Your Westie Along on Vacation

Before You Leave:
- ☐ Find out the requirements for taking the dog along on the train, plane, or ship; inquire about accommodations
- ☐ Ask about customs regulations
- ☐ Get a valid international vaccination certificate if you are traveling abroad; if required, get a health certificate (the auto clubs, American Veterinary Medical Association, or the embassy of the country concerned can give you information on requirements)
- ☐ Get a carrier, or plan to use the customary sleeping basket
- ☐ Get a muzzle (required in many countries)
- ☐ Get an adjustable pet vent for your car window if you are taking your own car, or get a safety harness for your dog
- ☐ Prepare a collar with your home address and vacation address

Have Handy During the Trip:
- ☐ Vaccination certificate and health certificate
- ☐ Leash and muzzle (in countries that require a muzzle)
- ☐ Drinking water and water dish
- ☐ Plastic bag or roll of paper towels to dispose of feces

Pack in Your Luggage:
- ☐ Dog food and food dish
- ☐ Can opener and spoon
- ☐ Brush and currying brush
- ☐ Sleeping basket or blanket
- ☐ Toys
- ☐ Small portable medicine case (your veterinarian can advise you)
- ☐ A few old cloths
- ☐ Policy number of your dog's liability insurance

longer at that age, but their activeness remains unchanged. Their sight and hearing are on the decline, although that presents no real problem for a dog, which uses its sense of smell to get its bearings. After your Westie's tenth year of life, you need to have it routinely examined by the veterinarian when the annual booster shots are due.

The Final Trip to the Veterinarian

As long as there is any hope of recovery, I continue to have my sick Westies treated. However, once all hope is gone, it is distinctly selfish to let the animal suffer simply because you want to spend a few more days with it. Put your little friend out of its discomfort, and remember that it is your duty to do your pet one last service of friendship: Stay with the Westie as it is given the final injection and goes to sleep. Ask your veterinarian whether he or she would come to your home to put the dog to sleep. I assure you, you will cope better with your pet's death if you know that it fell asleep peacefully and unafraid in your arms.

Proper Nutrition

A little companion of this kind needs a balanced diet that also contains vitamins and minerals.

For your Westie's growth, well-being, and continued good health—particularly in old age—it is extremely important that the dog be fed properly, that is, appropriately.

It is decidedly inappropriate to feed your dog by making it eat leftovers from your own table. Moreover, the nutritional requirements of humans and dogs are so very different that we are not able to provide a dog with the necessary nutrient levels through our culinary skills alone.

Appropriate Nutrition

Eating food meant for humans will result in nutritional deficiency symptoms in a dog, because its requirements for protein, carbohydrates, fats, vitamins, and minerals are quite different from ours. It would be equally inappropriate to feed a dog nothing but muscle meat. The dog's digestive system and metabolism resemble that of its ancestor, the wolf, and are geared to digest and utilize small, plant-eating animals. These prey animals are devoured to the last morsel, including the sinews, ligaments, bones, and the prey's stomach and intestines which contain undigested chyme, consisting largely of plant matter. In this way the dog's body obtains roughage, protein, carbohydrates, fats, minerals (such as calcium and phosphorus), vitamins, and trace elements.

Developing good eating habits. You should try to feed your puppy at the same time each day and at the same place, so that a routine that is advantageous to both pet and owner is established. Do not feed human food to your dog, because it will either provide empty calories that your pet doesn't need at all or, at best, will upset the nutritional balance that has been planned for it.

The Right Amount of Food and the Right Shape

The amount of food required daily varies from one Westie to another. It depends on the dog's level of activity, its age, and its opportunity for exercise.

A Westie normally weighs between 17 and 22 pounds (8–10 kg). Whether your Westie's figure is all it should be is something you can find out yourself. If the dog's ribs are palpable but do not protrude, your Westie is in ideal shape. The animal is too thin if its spinal column can be felt easily and its hipbones jut out. And you need to put your pet on a diet if, while the Westie is seated, you can pinch a thick roll of fat at the base of its tail. Cut back on your dog's daily rations, eliminate all "special treats" (see page 36), and see that it gets more exercise (see Keeping Your Dog Physically Fit, pages 38 and 39).

Where and When to Feed Your Westie

Dogs, like humans, like to enjoy their meals in peace and quiet. Always feed your pet at the same place, a spot where it can eat undisturbed. Fresh tap water, too, always needs to be available at the same place and accessible to the dog around the clock, so that it can drink whenever it likes.

These two have a good understanding: The dog is the child's playmate and partner.

Puppies between eight weeks and six months old should be given three meals a day: in the morning, at midday, and in the early evening. After the six-month mark two feedings a day are enough, until the dog is one year old; then feed it only once a day.

Young dogs need more protein and minerals in their diet than adult dogs. Special puppy food is available in pet stores. When you cut back from three meals a day to two or one, your Westie's own particular requirements have to be taken into account. If you feel that your pet still needs an additional meal fairly frequently, then provide it.

Make a practice of observing fixed mealtimes, so that the dog gets used to eating at those times. I like to feed my pets at midday, because then I can be certain that the dogs will have a chance to do their "business" before bedtime comes.

Commercial Dog Food

Commercial dog food has many advantages: It is quick and easy to prepare, and it contains everything a dog needs: The pet food industry, through long years of research, has determined the optimum composition of dog food.

Commercial dog food is marketed in three forms: moist, semimoist, and dry. You can buy kibbled combinations and vegetable combinations to add to the moist food, and the variety of between-meal snacks is truly enormous. All breeders advocate certain products on the basis of their many years of experience, and they will be happy to tell you what dog foods they recommend.

Moist or canned dog food is a nutritionally complete food that contains all the nutrients and substances essential to normal metabolism. The water content is 75 percent. Two types are available:

• Dog food that consists primarily of meat and/or protein-containing raw materials (muscle meats, tripe, heart, liver, and lungs).

• Dog food that has added carbohydrates in the form of grains (rice, barley, oats, wheat, or corn). You should always mix canned dog food with vegetable flakes or kibbled ration (⅔ moist food, ⅓ flakes), so that your Westie will not develop diarrhea.

Semimoist and dry dog foods are considerably more concentrated and higher in energy than canned dog food. They contain much less moisture: 10 to 20 percent for dry dog food and 25 to 30 percent for semimoist dog food. Consequently, dry dog food takes water away from the dog's body and places stress on the kidneys if the dog doesn't drink enough water. For this reason, you need to provide your pet with plenty of fresh drinking water.

Tip: I feed my Westies a well-balanced, nutritionally complete food that is 40 percent meat. Contrary to the manufacturer's recommendation, however, I don't add warm water to it

and stir. Instead, I prepare a meat broth (3.5 ounces [100 g] of finely chopped meat per Westie), add it to the complete food, and stir to form a mush. My dogs like the taste better.

As a change from the complete food, I give my Westies dry dog food that I have softened in some meat broth for 30 minutes. By moistening the food, I make sure that the dogs get enough liquid in their diet.

Until my Westies are 20 months old, they get a daily calcium supplement (the amount depends on the individual product).

What to Look for in a Dog Food

When you shop, make sure to get dog food in small quantities (4.5–11 pounds [2–5 kg]). Once the bag of dog food has been opened, it should be used as quickly as possible, because vitamins and minerals deteriorate over time.

In addition, the dog food you choose should contain preservatives in the form of vitamin combinations.

Drinking Water Is Important

Your Westie needs to have fresh, cool water available in the same place at all times. Dogs need milk only during the puppy stage—up to about the eighth week of life.

Adult dogs are unable to digest lactose, the sugar in milk, and they get diarrhea. Even skin diseases may result.

Bones for Your Westie

For the care and upkeep of your Westie's teeth, it is extremely important that the dog have something to gnaw. That is one method of largely preventing tartar formation. Particularly if you give your dog mostly soft dog food, you need to offset that by providing rawhide, hard dog biscuits, or bones. Don't let your pet have bones more than once a week. The best choices are joints of large veal and

Typical Westie!
Westies are not inclined to put on too much weight, but they can't resist treats. Don't over-do the extra bits of food, or your dog will have "little rolls of fat."

34

Rules for Feeding

- Always feed your Westie at the same time of day.
- Let the dog eat undisturbed.
- After every meal, clean the food dish thoroughly with hot water, to prevent buildup of harmful bacteria and fungi.
- Remove any uneaten food after about 30 minutes. It will turn sour and, if eaten, cause diarrhea. In summer it will attract flies.
- From the very start, get your Westie used to eating whatever you put before it. If you offer the dog something else every time it turns up its nose, it will soon just pick out the bits it likes and leave the rest. The result will be an unbalanced diet that is not conducive to good health.
- The dog food should be neither too hot nor too cold. If in doubt, test the temperature with your finger.
- Fresh water has to be available at all times.

Don't feed your dog the following:

- **Sweets.** They will lead to obesity and can damage the Westie's teeth.
- **Milk.** It causes diarrhea in many dogs. After the puppy has been weaned by its mother (between the sixth and eighth weeks of life), it no longer needs milk.

beef bones, so-called ball joints. Boiled oxtails are useful also. They should always be boiled first, to kill any bacteria, viruses, or parasites that may be present.

Generally speaking, don't give your dogs bones from animals other than those listed above. Pork, game, and poultry bones splinter and can cause injuries in the esophagus and rectal area.

Remember: If your dog eats too many bones, it will develop constipation, with rock-hard feces. In extreme cases, intestinal obstruction is the result.

Home-prepared Meals for Your Dog

Commercial dog food is an excellent source of nourishment for your dog.

Nevertheless, quite a few dog owners want to prepare meals for their pets themselves. They need to know the following: The basic nutrients—protein, fats, and carbohydrates—have to be supplied in the correct proportions, and the necessary vitamins and minerals have to be added. Moreover, all the amounts have to be properly gauged, so that the dog doesn't get too thin or too fat.

That may sound simple, but in practice it is not so easy to accomplish— quite apart from all the time you have to devote to cooking. Nonetheless, if you are interested in preparing meals for your pet, you need to keep the following information in mind:

Protein is contained primarily in meat, fish, farmer's cheese, and cottage cheese, in addition to certain plants like soybeans.

So-called essential amino acids, which the Westie's body does not produce itself, are present chiefly in animal protein. They have to be supplied along with the dog's food.

Always make sure that the meat you feed your dog has been cooked. Pork, as well as beef, should never be fed raw to your dog because of the danger of transmitting disease (toxoplasmosis and other diseases, see page 45). With raw poultry, there is a threat of salmonella.

Carbohydrates are found predominantly in grain, kibbled dog foods, rice, potatoes, and corn, as well as in cereal products such as noodles and bread. They are easily digestible, and, particularly in the case of whole-wheat products, they supply the body with important minerals and vitamins.

Fats are the body's chief source of energy, because they contain twice the calories of carbohydrates and protein.

Some fats are also present in meat. The so-called essential fatty acids are found principally in vegetable fats and oils. As the dog's body is able to produce only some of these acids, they need to be added to its food.

Minerals, trace elements, and vitamins are "vital substances," particularly important for young and old dogs.

If you add vitamin-enriched kibbled dog food to your pet's diet, there is no need to use vitamin and mineral supplements. Mixtures of these substances are available in pet stores and from veterinarians.

Average daily requirements of a healthy, full-grown Westie: about 7 ounces (200 g) of protein, 3.5 ounces (100 g) of carbohydrates, ½–1 teaspoon of oil, and a pinch of vitamin and mineral suplement.

Preparation: Let all the cooked ingredients cool completely, then mix them with the other components of the meal.

Feeding an Old Westie

We call a Westie "old" once it has reached its tenth birthday. Because the dog is becoming less active and its liver, kidneys, and intestines function less efficiently than those of a young animal, your pet requires high-carbohydrate, moderately low protein foods, which are easier to digest. In terms of your dog's needs, that means less meat, more rice and vegetables.

Ready-to-serve food for senior dogs is available commercially. It satisfies all the important nutritional requirements, and it is specially formulated for the needs of aging dogs.

If Your Westie Is Overweight

Westies belong to a breed that is not given to overeating. If you give your pet too generous a serving, it will leave some food uneaten in the bowl. Westies have a weakness, however, for "special tidbits," and a surplus of them is the most common cause of your pet's little rolls of fat. Cut out the special treats and reduce by 20 percent

This puppy is sniffing curiously at an apple.

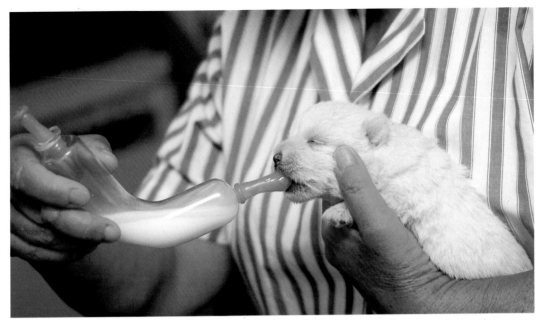

Rearing a puppy on the bottle is no longer a problem, thanks to the availability of milk replacers for puppies.

the amount you feed your Westie. If you can't resist the pleading look in its eyes, buy commercially prepared diet food from your veterinarian or in a pet store. Then your Westie can keep eating its customary amount of food, but be sure not to give it any extras. In about two months, your dog will shed four to five pounds, and you can resume normal feeding.

Always remember: Being overweight shortens your Westie's life expectancy.

Digestive Upsets

When something is wrong with your pet's stomach or bowels, vomiting and diarrhea usually result.

Let your Westie fast for a day, offering it, or administering to it, only cool water that has been boiled.

On the second day put it on the following diet, which is high in carbohydrates (about 70 percent), low in protein (about 30 percent), and very low in fat.

• Boil three peeled potatoes in salt water until done. Mash them, with a little salt water added, to a paste. Because of the diarrhea, your Westie's body loses salt, which you need to replace.

• Add some cottage cheese to the mashed potatoes and stir.

After two days, the dog's feces should be firm once again. If not, you need to see the veterinarian without further delay.

HOW-TO:
Keeping Your Dog Physically Fit

Westies are extremely agile dogs, full of energy and vitality, not satisfied with merely being walked around the block. They want to have their legs in motion as often as possible. And because they are also intelligent dogs, they enjoy learning as they play and carrying out

1. As you make your way through the obstacle course, your Westie also has to jump through a tire.

tasks—that is, staying "mentally" fit as well. Don't worry about asking too much of your dog. The problem with most dogs today is that they have too little to do; they are "underemployed." After all, the Westie's ancestors were hunting dogs, and as such they had a great deal to learn and difficult work to perform.

Walking

Walking is the essence of staying fit—for humans and dogs alike. If, for your dog's sake, you are forced to take at least one hour-long walk every day, whatever the weather, you soon will notice that you're doing yourself a favor as well; your heart and circulatory system will be on an even keel, and colds will become increasingly rare.

Minimum: one hour of walking per day. The walk is necessary even if you have a yard available for your Westie. Racing around the yard is no substitute for contact with the outside world. On its stroll through the neighborhood, your pet will pick up information—in large part by sniffing at everything—and meet other dogs. If you don't have a yard where the dog can run, you need to schedule two or three long walks, in addition to taking the Westie out several times just to do its "business." In your home or in the yard, you can give your pet some additional exercise by throwing a ball or a small stick. Appropriate toys are shown in Drawing 3.

Dog Sports

If you are willing to work, as well as walk, with your Westie, many types of dog sports will give you an opportunity to do so. For a bundle of energy like the Westie, sport means play. The local dog clubs near your home will give you information about training your Westie through recreational activities.

Agility
Drawings 1 and 2
Agility originated in England. In this country it is a relatively new type of sport for dogs and humans. Most dog play areas, however, now are equipped for it.

Obstacle course. The owner runs with his or her dog through a course equipped with various obstacles. The Westie jumps over small hurdles or through tires. It runs up an inclined plank, crosses over a second, level, plank about 5 feet (1.5 m) off the ground, then runs down a third plank on the opposite side. In the slalom, it has to weave in and out of a series of upright poles without skipping any. Walking across a seesaw or through a fabric tunnel takes courage.

Obedience and trust. The dog has to obey readily if it is to engage in competition with other dogs. In contests, the animal has to negotiate the obstacle course within a certain time, in a sequence announced by the judge just before the meet begins. After every station on the course, the dog has to wait for a signal from its master or mistress before proceeding, not just spontaneously attempt any obstacle it chooses. For this to succeed, the dog has to trust "its" human.

Flyball

This new team sport for dogs originated in the United States. Directed by their owners, the dogs race through an obstacle course. All dogs are allowed to participate, regardless of age and breed. A Westie can easily have a German shepherd as a teammate.

The rules: Two teams of four dogs apiece take parallel positions at the starting line. Every dog has to cover a distance of

2. *After running through the dark fabric tunnel, the dog gets a reward from its master or mistress.*

ping your pet's favorite treats every few yards.

Finding the scent. Once the dog's owner has vanished, your assistant should start walking, with the Westie on its long retractable leash.

The command "Seek" will signal the Westie to begin searching for the scent. It is all right to give the dog a little assistance at first, to keep it from losing the scent. Once the dog has found its master or mistress, shower it with praise.

The Westie enjoys the job of tracking, because it closely resembles its original work as a hunting dog. If you want to improve your dog's performance, you also can have it trained in your dog club as a tracker.

17.5 yards (16 m), clearing four hurdles, the height of which depends on the smallest jumping dog on the team. Then the dog is in front of the flyball box. It pushes the pedal with its paw, catches the tennis ball that flies out of the box, and goes the same 17.5 yards (16 m) back over the hurdles to the finish. As soon as one dog crosses the finish line, the next one starts.

The winning team is the one that completes the relay race first. Flyball takes some practice, because without training, the dog will stand helplessly in front of the ball container. It will soon learn its lesson, however, and the Westie and its master or mistress will enjoy the fun and excitement.

Track the Scent

To play "tracking," you don't have to go the dog club. All you need is a friend to help you and your pet.

How to play: Go to the woods with your Westie and a second person who is familiar to the dog. About 110 yards (100 m) from the woods' edge, the Westie and the other person stop. You should proceed into the woods and, once out of the dog's sight, turn and continue walking at a 90° angle to your previous direction of movement. After about 33 yards (30 m), hide behind a tree. The entire time, mark your trail by drop-

3. *Suitable toys: A toy to fetch, made of hardwood (1), rings to throw, made of solid rubber (2) and (6), solid rubber ball (3), shoe and bone, both made of rawhide (4) and (5), knotted rope to pull (7).*

What to Do If Your Westie Gets Sick

The Westie feels happy surrounded by "its" family. It always wants to be as close as possible to whatever is going on, and if danger threatens, it courageously positions itself in front of its loved ones.

If you purchase your Westie from a good breeder (see page 14)—one we hope that is affiliated with the American Kennel Club or the West Highland White Terrier Club of America—you will optimize your chances of having acquired a healthy, robust dog. Westies are not among the breeds that have been weakened by overbreeding. The only breed-related problem that may occur is craniomandibular osteopathy (CMO; see page 45).

How to Tell Whether Your Dog Is Ill

Dog owners who are familiar with their pets can tell by the dogs' behavior whether they are ill or not. If your dog no longer jumps up with its normal enthusiasm when you suggest taking a walk, or if it creeps away and hides, or refuses to eat, it may be showing symptoms of an illness, and these symptoms have to be explored thoroughly. Your veterinarian will stand by with help and advice at all times (for information on canine diseases, see the list of books on page 62).

How the Dog Owner Can Help

Keep a first aid kit handy. There are accidents and health problems that owners can deal with in the same manner they do with their children. A first aid kit should contain adhesive tape, hydrogen peroxide, medicated powder, gauze bandages, cotton applicator swabs, tweezers, and a thermometer. All minor cuts should be handled by the owner, who will stop the bleeding, clean the cut with the peroxide, apply the ointment with the swab, and cover the wound with a light bandage. Do not apply wads of cotton to a wound because they will stick to it and may cause contamination. The bandage should be light to let in as much air as possible to the wound. The tweezers will come in handy for removing foreign objects from the dog's throat, ears, or skin.

Taking the dog's temperature. Contrary to popular belief, a hot, dry nose is not an indication that the dog has fever. The presence of an elevated temperature can be determined only by feeling the lower abdomen or the insides of the thighs. If these areas feel unusually warm, although the dog is not worn out and has not been racing around, you need to take its temperature. To do so, use a slender, nonbreakable thermometer; models with a digital display and a signaling beep are best, because they give the fastest read-out. Lubricate the tip of the thermometer with vaseline. While keeping the dog in a standing position—have someone help you, if possible—raise your pet's tail and insert the thermometer, at a slight upward angle, about 1.2 inches (3 cm) in its anus. A conventional stubby rectal thermometer needs to stay in place for two to three minutes. A digital thermometer can be removed after only one minute or as soon as you hear the beep. If the Westie's temperature is over 102.5°F (39°C), the dog has a fever. Subnormal temperature (under

Only on property that is securely fenced in can you unleash your Westie and play with it without having to worry.

To take your pet's temperature, lift its tail and carefully insert the thermometer in its anus.

100.4°F [38°C] also can be a symptom of illness.

Taking the dog's pulse. If you suspect that the Westie is ill, you also need to check its pulse. The best place for that is the midportion of the inner side of the upper thigh. If you press gently there with your fingertips, you will feel the pulsing of the femoral artery. A Westie's normal pulse rate is 100 to 120 beats per minute.

Administering medicine. It is easiest to administer liquid medications in a disposable syringe (minus the needle), which you can get in a pharmacy or from your veterinarian. Insert the syringe at the side of the dog's mouth, between its teeth. Lift the animal's head slightly and, with its mouth closed, slowly squirt the liquid onto its tongue, so that the dog will be forced to swallow it (see drawing, page 46). If

you have someone helping you, it will be even easier.

If the medicine is in tablet form, conceal the tablets in a treat like cheese or liverwurst. Make sure the Westie doesn't spit the medicine out again. If that method fails, open the dog's mouth, place the tablet far back on the tongue, and close its mouth; it has to swallow the bitter pill whether it wants to or not. Then, using a syringe, you can give the Westie some water to help the tablet go down more easily.

A suppository needs to be lubricated with some Vaseline after you have removed it from its wrapping. Then, with your (gloved) finger, push it as deep as possible into the dog's anus. Next, press your finger over the anus for a short time.

What the Veterinarian Needs to Know

To properly diagnose and treat a sick dog, it is crucial that the veterinarian get ample and precise information from you. Ideally, write down what you have observed. Note how long the Westie has had certain symptoms, and try to describe as exactly as possible how they present themselves (for example, the dog's posture when it experiences or shows evidence of perceiving certain pains, or the nature of the dog's cough) and in what situations they occur.

The following list will give you a basis for deciding what you need to report to the veterinarian:
• When and what did your dog last drink or eat?
• When did it last urinate or defecate? Did it have any difficulty doing so?
• What was the stool like? Note color, hard or soft consistency, any admixture of blood or mucus; possibly bring along a sample. Was there any blood in the urine?
• Has the dog vomited? How often, how much, and what? Look for blood

Typical Westie!

It wants to do physical and mental "work." It likes various kinds of dog sports, and its master and mistress are welcome to take an active part in them.

and foreign objects, and bring a sample if possible.
• Does the dog suffer from flatulence or display evidence of a stomachache?
• Does it sneeze, cough, drool, or gag?
• Does it have fever? How high? (See also page 40.)
• Does your dog hobble or limp? How long has it been doing so, and in what situations? Does it stand with its back arched? Does it have a stiff-legged gait? Does it have trouble getting on its feet?
• Does the dog stop when it comes to stairs, or does it refuse to jump onto the sofa or into the car?
• Does it lick, scratch, or bite certain areas of its body? Does it scoot along on its bottom ("sledding") and try to lick its tail?
• Does it frequently shake its head and scratch its ears?

• Does it react by expressing pain (whimpering, crying out, or even biting) when certain body parts are touched?

Preventive Medicine: Immunizations and Worming

Regular worming treatments and vaccinations are the most important preventive measures you can take to keep your pet healthy.

Immunizations. The appointments for your routine visits to the veterinarian are based on the vaccination schedule (see below). It is critical that you follow that schedule and that the dog receive its shots regularly! An unprotected animal can contract infectious diseases that may prove fatal, and some of them are communicable to humans (see Important Notes, page 63).

Immunization Schedule

The veterinarian will give your Westie a vaccination certificate when it has its first inoculation. Taking the date of the last inoculation as a guide, use the following schedule for planning appointments:
• Puppies are first inoculated at the age of eight to nine weeks. (In populations with parvovirosis problems, however, give the first inoculation at the age of five to seven weeks.) The little Westie gets its second inoculation when 12 to 14 weeks old.
• Full-grown dogs are inoculated on an annual basis. Because immunity to distemper and hepatitis lasts for two years, the series of five inoculations is followed the next year by a series of three. To be on the safe side where immunity is concerned, veterinarians recently have begun to urge that the series of five be given annually.

Worming Schedule

Puppies need to be wormed at these ages: two, four, six, eight, and 12 weeks, and six and nine months. For an adult Westie, worming is necessary twice a year. If your dog digs for mice or has fleas, have it wormed more frequently; fleas are carriers of the dog tapeworm.

It is important that one of the treatments be given before an inoculation is scheduled, so that the dog is completely free from worms when it gets its shots.

Because there are various kinds of worms, you need to use a worm remedy with as broad a spectrum of action as possible. Ask your veterinarian to recommend one. Not all pet shops and pharmacists are adequately informed about such treatments. Moreover, many of these remedies have to be prescribed by a veterinarian.

This Westie serenely puts up with the veterinarian's examination.

Dogs are inoculated against rabies, distemper, hepatitis, parvovirosis, leptospirosis, and "kennel cough." Because immunity to these diseases is not lifelong, it is extremely important that the inoculations be repeated at regular intervals, through your pet's life. Young Westies are particularly susceptible, because their immune systems are not yet fully developed. Old dogs, too, are at risk, and it would be foolish to discontinue your pet's immunizations once it reaches a certain age.

Worming. Regular worming is necessary for two reasons: First, a dog that is weakened by worm infestation is more susceptible to infections; second, worms can also be transmitted to humans. Children in particular are at risk (see Important Notes, page 63).

Parasites

Even the best-groomed Westie comes in contact with fleas or ticks.

Examine your pet as you brush it, so that you can do something about the parasites if necessary.

Flea collars, available in pet stores or from your veterinarian, give some degree of protection against fleas. Tablets and tinctures, also available commercially, have a preventive effect. I advise against their use, however, because they harm not only the vermin, but your Westie as well.

Ticks. They are active only in the warmer months of the year. With their mouthparts, ticks take a firm hold on your dog's skin and suck their fill of its blood. You can remove a tick by grasping its rear part with tweezers or special tick nippers and twisting to dislodge it from the puncture site. When you pull the tick out, don't leave its head and jaws behind. Inflammation can result.

Ticks can also transmit diseases such as borreliosis (Lyme Disease), an infectious disease that in many cases causes joint inflammation in dogs and humans.

Fleas. If your Westie scratches itself frequently, it may have fleas. One sure symptom of flea infestation is the presence of flea droppings in your pet's fur: tiny, dark specks that leave red spots on a damp white cloth. Apply flea powder, then repeat the procedure after one week. In addition, spray your dog's bed and the area surrounding its favorite place. Spray again one week later, when the new generation of fleas is hatching. Although fleas are not carriers of disease, they are intermediate hosts for tapeworms. If your dog eats a flea, it may acquire a tapeworm. For this reason, a dog that has fleas also needs to be wormed.

Aujeszky's Disease

The cause of Aujeszky's disease is a virus that occurs chiefly in pigs. If pork is stored together with beef, the virus may spread to the beef. Dogs become infected primarily by consuming undercooked pork. The disease is fatal in dogs, but not contagious for humans. Fortunately, it is relatively rare.

The symptoms are copious drooling, itching, restlessness, and anxiety. If this disease is suspected, see a veterinarian at once.

Craniomandibular Osteopathy

Luckily, this bone disease, which occurs in puppyhood, is rare. During the growth phase, the bone cells of the jaw and/or the skull multiply at an unnaturally fast rate. The result is an often palpable thickening of the bone. The puppy is in great pain when it is touched or when it chews.

Craniomandibular osteopathy (CMO) appears at the time the puppy is getting its teeth, approximately between the second and the eighth months of life.

Once all the teeth are in—after about the ninth month—the disease comes to a halt, and the Westie can lead a completely normal life.

The symptoms are sensitivity to having its head touched, lack of appetite, lethargy. Diagnosis is possible only with the help of x-rays.

Many veterinarians give the puppy cortisone, which I find problematic, because this medication affects the growth of all the bones.

The most important thing during the course of the disease is that the puppy get enough to eat. If it is given very soft food that it doesn't have to chew, it will eat.

If the pain is severe, you can give the dog tiny doses of a pain remedy (aspirin) before it eats.

CMO as a hereditary disease. Once this disease appears, the parents should never be bred again, nor should the puppy ever be bred.

The problem is that the disease breaks out only if both parents are carriers of CMO. If only one parent is afflicted, the disease will not appear. Fifty percent of the puppies resulting from these parents' mating, however, will be CMO carriers.

Soon it will be back on its feet again.

45

HOW-TO:
First Aid

Accidents happen all too quickly. Once an accident has occurred, your dog is dependent on your ability to make the right decision and on the first aid you can provide. Keep calm, and think before you act. After you do what you can, however, you need to get your Westie to a veterinarian immediately.

1. *In case of poisoning, administer a concentrated solution of table salt and water, using a syringe without a needle.*

Poisoning
Drawing 1

Signs of poisoning are frequent vomiting, copious drooling, and occasionally diarrhea as well; blood may be present in the stool, urine, or vomit; the mucous membranes may be pale; and the dog is apathetic. Stumbling, convulsions, symptoms of paralysis, and loss of consciousness can result.

Consequences of poisoning: The type of poison the dog has picked up determines whether it

can be saved. If you know what your Westie has eaten (antifreeze, sedatives, insecticides, rat poison), tell the veterinarian immediately. If you saw your Westie eating the poison, you need to empty the contents of its stomach at once. Your Westie's chances for survival depend largely on how quickly you act. Gastric irrigation or purgatives can reduce the amount of poison in the dog's system only within the first 30 to 60 minutes.

Most important procedures if poisoning has occurred:
• Empty the stomach contents: Using a syringe without a needle, feed your Westie a concentrated salt water solution (one tablespoon of table salt to 3.4 ounces [100 ml] of water), to induce vomiting (for method of administering, see page 42). (see page 42)
• Get in touch with your veterinarian at once, and take your dog to his or her office as quickly as possible.
• Give the dog activated charcoal tablets—they won't do any harm. Charcoal absorbs most poisons.

• Make sure the dog drinks plenty of water. Water has a diluting effect, and, if the dog vomits after drinking, it will have almost the same effect as gastric irrigation.

Important: If poisoning is suspected, don't give the dog milk, oil, or castor oil; that might exacerbate the symptoms and complaints.

Insect Bites
It is completely impossible to break a Westie of snapping at flying insects. If your pet rubs its jaws on the ground or scratches its muzzle with its paw, it has been bitten or stung on the muzzle or in the mouth. If swelling in the throat area makes it extremely difficult for the dog to swallow and breathe, use ice cubes to cool down the area from the outside, then see the vet at once. If the Westie has been stung by several bees, wasps, or even hornets, you also need to see the veterinarian without delay, because allergic reactions such as vomiting, difficulty in breathing, and coughing fits may result.

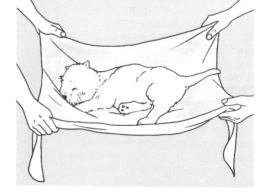

2. *An injured dog can be transported carefully on a blanket.*

If the Westie was stung on the foot, take a look at the place; if it was a bee, the stinger will still be in the paw. Remove it, then cool the place with ice cubes.

Accidents
Drawing 2

Transporting the dog to the veterinarian. If your Westie has been hit by a car or a bicycle, it has to be taken to the veterinarian at once. Because you never know whether any bones are broken or any internal injuries are present, it is important to transport the dog lying down. It would be ideal to place it on a board, although one is not likely to be available at the accident site. Make do with a coat or a blanket. If you have someone to help you, the two of you can lift the Westie, lying on its blanket, and put it in the car.

First aid. If the dog is unconscious, make sure its respiratory passages stay open. Open its mouth, pull out its tongue, and place it between its teeth on one side. It is essential to keep the mouth clear of vomit, because the dog would choke on it. Any pulsating bleeding has to be stopped. Tie the leg above the heel and/or elbow with a tourniquet of elastic material (nylon stocking, sock). This emergency dressing serves only to keep the dog from bleeding to death en route to the veterinarian. If the trip to the veterinarian's office takes more than 30 minutes, the tourniquet has to be loosened briefly from time to time, to keep the leg from becoming gangrenous.

If the injury is in a place that cannot be ligated (for example,

3. If a paw is cut, use a compress and a bandage to create a pressure dressing.

in the chest or the abdominal area), you need to exert pressure on the vessel with your hand and a clean, dry compress to stop the bleeding.

Cuts on the Paws
Drawing 3

Foot injuries bleed profusely. The first thing to do is to stop the bleeding. Remove any dirt

and foreign objects from the wound, and apply a pressure dressing. If you are in a busy part of town, you can ask a taxi driver to give you a gauze bandage and a compress from his or her first-aid box. [Note: Some state laws require that such a kit be carried in every taxi.] Lay the compress directly on the wound and wrap it tightly with the bandage. If you have no bandaging materials available, cover the cut with a clean handkerchief and wrap a sock or a scarf around the foot. If the wound is bleeding severely, apply a make-shift tourniquet to the leg (see left column, this page) and drive immediately to the veterinarian's office.

Important: In any case, cuts on the paw require a veterinarian's treatment. Because the paw continually comes in contact with dirt, any wound that is not sutured (or adequately bandaged) can fester and take weeks to heal.

Bites

Even if a fight that involved biting seems to have ended without injury, you need to examine your Westie thoroughly. Otherwise, bite wounds in its thick fur may go unnoticed and turn into abscesses. Take care of any wounds that are bleeding heavily (see Accidents), then drive to the veterinarian's office immediately. Often the opponent's canine tooth has pierced the skin and left a perforation. Although the wound is small and bleeds little, it must be treated by a veterinarian. Dirt has gotten under the skin, and an abscess may form, even days after the dogs' fight. If that happens, the Westie will be apathetic, stop eating, and develop fever or even blood poisoning.

Westies are extremely agile as well as intelligent. They enjoy learning as they play and carrying out little tasks. Dog sports offer owners a wide range of opportunities to get exercise along with their four-legged friends. In addition, playing with your dog deepens the understanding between dog and human.

Breeding Westies

There is a widespread misconception that every male has to mate and every female has to bear a litter, to preclude emotional problems or diseases. Even among the dog's ancestors, the wolves, however, only the strongest females reproduced, while the others saw to raising the puppies. Among the males, too, only the alpha males—the best in the pack—got the chance to sire a litter. That means your Westie can lead a normal, healthy, happy life without becoming a father or mother. It is up to you whether you use the animal for breeding. If that is your intention, however, you need to keep the following in mind.

Economics of Breeding

Many owners start a breeding program because they see a financial

As they suckle, puppies press their paws against their mother's abdomen and stimulate milk production.

reward at the end. If so, please consider the time and money involved to get your bitch into breeding condition, to sustain her through pregnancy, and house, feed, and housebreak the puppies. Additional expenses will inevitably erode your budget, including continuous trips to the veterinarian for checkups, inoculations, wormings, and medications, as well as the cost and chore of advertising and showing the puppies at all hours of the week. Of the many owners who have tried breeding, a few managed to break even and only a minuscule number could make a living out of it.

Responsibility for Breeding

When it comes to breeding, only the best will do. Westies with anatomical faults or poor character traits are not suitable for breeding. The defects of one partner cannot be offset by the merits of the other, because the sum total of the genes transmitted from parents to offspring will have an effect on the puppies.

Even if you want to let your female mate just once, you need time, money, the right place, and specialized knowledge. You can get specialized books or articles dealing with the raising of puppies, or you can take your questions to the West Highland White Terrier Club of America (see Addresses, page 63). The Club's breeding supervisor responsible for your local area will help you free of charge.

Breeding Regulations

Pedigree. You should breed only a Westie that is registerable with the American Kennel Club and that has no serious faults or genetic anomalies.

Breeding regulations. Chapter 3 Section 5 of the American Kennel Club's Rules Applying to Registration reads: "No dog or litter out of a dam under eight months or over twelve years of age at the time of mating, or by a sire under seven months or over twelve years of age at the time of mating, will be registered unless the application for registration shall be accompanied by an affidavit or evidence which shall prove the fact to the satisfaction of the American Kennel Club."

In my breeding program, I use a female only up to her fifth or, at most, sixth year of life. The ideal time for her first mating is between the second and third year of life. If females are older than that when they bear their first litter, considerable difficulties often accompany the birth.

Intervals between pregnancies. They are required for the female, and the length of the interval depends on the number of puppies in the litter.

The Love Life of a Male Dog

Unlike female dogs, males are ready to breed at all times. That will become apparent to you if a female in season is in the vicinity. If that is the case, and your male howls day and night and refuses to eat, talk to your veterinarian. Homeopathic remedies may help alleviate your pet's lovesick condition.

The Female in Heat

Female dogs come into heat twice a year. The first heat, or estrus, occurs when the dog is between five and seven months old. After that, she will be "in heat" approximately every six months. Only during the estrus season, which lasts for three weeks, is she ready to mate. This period of sexual receptivity can be broken down into three phases: proestrus, estrus (the estrous peak), and metestrus (post-estrus).

Studs

If you own only one or two bitches, it makes more sense not to keep your own stud, but to use males belonging to other breeders. If you want to keep both male and female Westies, you need to have enough room to keep them separated while the bitch is in season.

To find a suitable stud, you can visit dog shows and talk to other breeders, as well as review the stud issues of two publications, *Terrier Type* and *Westie Imprint* (for addresses, see p. 62). The male should not have a close "genetic connection" to your bitch; that is, he should not share too closely the same bloodlines as the female. Then you can be certain that the puppies will resemble their parents without being too closely inbred.

• During the proestrus phase, the female bleeds lightly at first, and the blood is dark. She licks herself clean, so that her condition goes virtually unnoticed. Males are already interested in her, but she rebuffs their advances.
• Once the female's peak phase begins, the blood becomes lighter in color; the bleeding lessens or ceases altogether. You can recognize this phase by the fact that the female's vulva is swollen and she immediately moves her tail to one side when you stroke its base.

The period of possible conception usually coincides with the midpoint of her season.

• During estrus, you can buy your female Westie sanitary garments and pads, available in pet stores. Then she can continue to move around freely indoors, without leaving any

Typical Westie!
Wherever a Westie's head will fit, the rest of its body will follow. Your property needs to be surrounded by an "escape-proof" fence.

spots of blood on the carpet or a favorite armchair.

A female in heat releases urine to attract male dogs. If you carry your female for a short distance, the dogs outside will be unable to follow her scent all the way to your front door.

If a male approaches you during this critical period while you're out for a walk, pick up your female Westie. That will prevent unwanted offspring.

Mating

For the space of a few days, the female is sexually receptive. If she mates with several different males during this time, the litter may include puppies sired by different fathers.

During the mating act, the male's penis and the bulbous cavernous body at the base of his penis become enlarged, while the female's vaginal ring constricts—the dogs are "stuck" together. That may last 15 to 30 minutes. Under no circumstances should you try to separate animals engaged in an unplanned act of mating. For anatomical reasons, your efforts are bound to fail.

Also make sure that the female does not sit down or cause serious injury to herself and the male by making a sudden swiveling motion.

Among breeders it is customary for the female to come to the home of the male when mating is to take place. By this time the necessary formalities, such as inspecting the papers, determining what stud fee the male's owner will receive, and specifying how often the male will be available for service, should already have been taken care of.

After mating has occurred, give the female a day to rest, then take her back to the male. The probability that she will conceive is increased.

Pregnancy

The female dog's period of gestation is 58 to 65 days after each mating.

When can we finally start? A Westie looking forward to a game. Let your dog persuade you to play as often as possible. It will keep you fit as well.

Count 58 days from the first mating and 65 from the last. Mark this range on your calendar as the likely time frame for whelping, and don't make any other plans for those days.

If the bitch has conceived, she will be somewhat quieter and more affectionate.

After estrus, the swelling of her genitals does not disappear completely. There is a slight discharge of mucus, and her nipples become enlarged. In about the fifth week, you can tell that her little belly is becoming rounded. The bitch's daily routine should not be altered. I take my pregnant Westies along on our 2-mile (3 km) walks up to the very end; we just move a little slower.

From the fourth week on, a pregnant bitch needs to eat twice her usual amount of food. Her diet should include plenty of minerals, trace elements, and vitamins. Especially toward the end of her pregnancy and during lactation, she needs additional minerals and calcium.

False Pregnancy

In a nonpregnant female, a kind of pseudopregnancy caused by hormones also may occur. Two months after heat—around the theoretical whelping date—the female begins to build an imaginary nest. She looks for a "baby substitute"—a stuffed animal, for example—places it next to her nipples, and produces milk. Such lactation had a real purpose among her pack-dwelling ancestors when female dogs were available as wet-nurses.

Remove the baby substitute. If the female's nipples are inflamed, take her to the veterinarian.

The Whelping Box

Equipment. The whelping box, made of wood, should be 16 inches (40 cm) high and 32 × 32 inches (80 × 80 cm) square.

A canine encounter: After nose contact comes the anal check.

Eight inches (20 cm) above the bottom, cut out an entrance. The mother has to be able to leave the whelping box easily, but the puppies must be kept from falling out.

Lay a brick in front of the entrance to serve as a step, so that the female doesn't injure her puppies or nipples by jumping into the box.

Make sure the whelping box is painted with environmentally safe wood varnish that does not produce any harmful vapors.

I put a blanket on the bottom of the box. Ideal for that purpose is the "drybed" sold in pet stores. On it, I spread out a skidproof mat measuring 32 × 32 inches (80 × 80 cm). On top of that I make a thin, solid layer of newspaper strips. They will absorb the urine and keep the dogs warm. Replace the strips daily. If you put down towels or blankets, the puppies may creep under them and be crushed to death by their mother.

Location. Put the whelping box in a room with a temperature of about 64.4°F (18°C). The puppies need to be protected from drafts. About 51 inches (1.30 m) above the box, attach an infrared heat lamp with a 150-watt bulb.

Birth

Initial contractions. The day before giving birth, most female dogs refuse to eat. They are restless, tremble, pant heavily, and start to dig an imaginary nest. The first stage of labor has begun. It can continue for many hours before changing into the final stage, when the dog bears down.

By all means let her move around in the whelping room during the preliminary phase; exercise will speed the delivery.

Final stage of labor. The dog's body convulses. The pains recur at increasingly short intervals. Fluid is discharged from the vagina. Soon after that, the first puppy appears, enclosed in the fetal membrane and the ring-shaped placenta.

Once the female has pressed out a puppy, she eats the fetal membrane and placenta and bites through the umbilical cord. Don't try to keep her from eating the afterbirth; the placenta contains hormones that accelerate the progress of the delivery and stimulate milk production. By licking the puppies clean, the mother gets their circulation going.

If there are complications:
Complications may occur at birth because of the size and the broad skulls of the Westie puppies.

You need to intervene if the puppy is only halfway out of the vagina and the mother stops bearing down. Take hold of the puppy's body with a towel. Moving the little creature gently back and forth, work it out of the vagina.

If the female doesn't tear open the fetal membrane immediately after the

Typical Westie!
It is an ideal playmate for children, with an affectionate, well-balanced disposition. Children have to learn, however, not to misuse their pet by treating it as a mere plaything.

Getting Ready for the Birth
• About four weeks before the due date, have the bitch wormed.
• From then on, give her two meals a day, including calcium and additional vitamins.
• A few days before the earliest possible due date, carefully clip the hair on the female's belly, to give the puppies better access to her nipples.
• Lay out towels, sterile (boiled) scissors, thread or dental floss, a kitchen scale, milk replacer for puppies, and a pet nurser or a dropper.
• From the 57th day on, take the dog's temperature regularly (see page 40). A drop in body temperature to 98.6°F (37°C) tells you that the birth is 24 to 36 hours away.

puppy's birth, you will have to open this wrapping near the puppy's head, to free its respiratory passages as quickly as possible. If you lift up the puppy to do so, you also need to hold the afterbirth, to which the animal is connected, in your hand, to keep its weight from tearing open the puppy's abdominal wall. With a towel, clean the head and muzzle. Then pull the fetal membrane off the body and sever the umbilical cord about .8 inch (2 cm) from the little abdomen.

Put the puppy face down in your hand and rub a towel over its back to stimulate its circulation. Keep rubbing until the puppy emits a cry; only then will it have enough air to survive.

If pulsating blood appears after you cut the umbilical cord, tie off the cord about .4 inch (1 cm) above the little belly, using the thread or dental floss that you placed ready in advance (see box, page 54).

The first swallow of milk. Right after birth, the puppy instinctively and unerringly heads for its mother's nipples. Carefully express a droplet of milk from the nipple to encourage the newborn to drink.

If the female still has no milk an hour after whelping, mix some milk replacer for puppies according to the manufacturer's instructions, and feed the puppy with a pet nurser or a dropper. If the opening in the nipple on the nurser bottle is too big, the puppy will choke, and there is a danger that it could die of pneumonia from inhaling milk replacer.

If the mother never begins to lactate, the puppy will need a bottle every two hours, around the clock.

The Puppies' Development

Puppies are born with a coat of fur. Their eyes and ears stay shut for about two weeks, but their sense of smell begins to function at once. During the first four weeks, the mother takes care of all the puppies' needs and keeps the whelping box scrupulously clean. While she is lactating, she needs twice her usual amount of food. Be sure to add calcium to her meals to prevent nutritional deficiency symptoms.

After about three weeks, the first clumsy attempts to walk are made. At four weeks, the puppies are pushing their way out of the whelping box.

It is crucial that you spend a great deal of time with the puppies between their third and seventh weeks of life. During that time they are in the imprinting phase. If they lack sufficient human contact, they will remain shy and have trouble relating to people.

At the ninth week, the socialization phase begins (see page 20). This is a good time to find new homes for the puppies.

Feeding the Puppies

After the fourth week, you should lessen your female dog's burden and feed the puppies four times a day. Give them a nutritionally complete food for puppies. I soften this complete food in broth made from boiled meat. At every fourth meal, I stir cottage cheese, instead of the meat broth, into the complete food. I add calcium to one of the four meals.

Don't forget to worm the puppies (see page 43) every two weeks, from the end of the second week until they go to new homes at the age of eight or nine weeks.

Puppies practice patterns of behavior while playing with their brothers and sisters.

Showing Your Westie

The American Kennel Club governs and administers competition in conformation and performance events, clubs that wish to hold them, and the individuals who exhibit and compete in the events. A potential exhibitor should obtain from the American Kennel Club their *Rules Applying to Dog Shows.*

Types of Shows

Specialty show: A Specialty Show is given by a club formed for the improvement of any one breed or purebred dogs. Championship points are awarded at this event.

All-breed show: Dogs of all breeds participate in this type of event held by member or licensed clubs. Championship points awarded are the same as those awarded at the Specialty Show.

Sanctioned match: A Sanctioned Match is an informal meeting at which purebred dogs compete. No championship points are awarded.

Championships: Championship points are recorded for Winners Dog and Winners Bitch at licensed and member dog shows approved by the American Kennel Club. Championship points are based on the number of eligible dogs competing in the regular classes of each sex in each breed. Any dog that wins fifteen points becomes a Champion. Six or more of said points shall have been won at two shows with a rating of three or more points under two different judges. The balance of points must be won under judges other than the two judges referred to above.

How Dogs Are Judged

Classes. In every breed of dogs, males are judged first, then bitches. For each sex there are five classes.

1. *Puppy,* for dogs between six months and one year of age.

2. *Novice,* for dogs which have never won a first prize.

3. *Bred by Exhibitor,* for all dogs except Champions, six months of age and older, which are owned and exhibited by the same person or kennel who are recognized breeders in the records of the American Kennel Club.

4. *American-bred,* for dogs born in the United States.

5. *Open,* for all dogs, American- and foreign-bred.

Usually the most experienced dog shows are to be seen in the American-bred and Open classes.

Winners class. Into this class come the first-prize winners of the above classes. Two awards are given: Winners (purple ribbon) and Reserve Winners (purple and white ribbon).

Best of Breed competition. Dogs of either sex which are already Champions. The two which were chosen Winners compete here and one is chosen Best of Breed. This dog competes later in the Groups as sole representative of its breed.

Best of Winners. Only two dogs compete in this class—the Winners Male and Winners Bitch. One is chosen Best of Winners.

Championship points. Championship points can be won by one dog and one bitch in each breed. The Winners dog and Winners bitch receive these points. The number

Naturally, every Westie owner thinks his or her own dog is the most beautiful of all. Owners have a chance to prove that publicly at dog shows, where the dogs are led before a judge. If your Westie wins, it will even be awarded a title.

depends on the number of each sex competing in each breed. When a dog has received 15 points it becomes a Champion and holds the title all its life.

Judges' criteria. As the judges go over each dog in the ring they are comparing it to a mental picture of the perfect dog of that breed. They judge each dog on:

1. Physical structure (head, feet, teeth, bone structure, muscle tone, etc.).

2. Condition (proper weight, condition of coat, animation, etc.).

3. Gait—as seen from front, side, and rear.

4. Temperament—penalizing heavily for shyness or viciousness.

The end of the show. In a dog show the competition becomes keener and more exciting at the end. When all breeds have been judged only one dog in each breed remains undefeated, the one which was chosen Best of Breed. These dogs are called to compete in one of seven groups: *Sporting, Hound, Working, Terrier, Toy, Non-sporting,* and *Herding.* One wins in each group. These seven Group Winners meet in the final competition and one is chosen Best in Show. This dog alone at the end remains undefeated.

Getting Ready for the Show Ring

Before you show your Westie, you first need to visit a show, become familiar with the set-up, and talk to other Westie exhibitors. Most will be willing to help. When you are showing a dog yourself, you need to know the following:

• American Kennel Club has information about show locations and dates.

• Entry forms are available from the show's organizers.

• You will need to pay an entry fee.

• You will need the AKC number of your dog, and the names of sire and dam.

• Although it is sufficient to trim a pet every three months, a show dog needs to be trimmed every two weeks. The trim has to be perfect, without making the Westie look unnatural and "overtrimmed" (see description of trimming, page 59).

• Westies are not only born to be champions, they are also trained to be champions. I start the show-training process during the puppy stage, by putting the dog on a table for its daily brushing. I conclude the brushing session with the correct "composition" for a Westie: raised head and erect tail. I also check its little teeth. The ceremony ends with a shower of praise.

• A show dog has to get used to environmental noise early on, so that it is not upset by the noise level common at a dog show. Because my Westies live in the peaceful countryside, surrounded by fields, I take them for walks and training classes.

• The evening before the show, give your Westie a shower in warm water.

• Some requirements are standard in all dog shows, whereas others change. Be thoroughly informed before the big day comes.

Trimming Before a Show
Drawing right

1. Start with the trimming knife right behind the dog's ears, plucking out as many hairs as necessary for the top coat to fit closely.

2. Continuing to work in that way, move from the nape across the shoulders, back, and sides to the tip of the tail.

3. Trim the upper side of the tail, and clip the feathery hairs on its underside with scissors. The sides of the tail also need to be cut short. The tail should taper to a point at the end and widen toward the base; it should somewhat resemble a carrot in shape. When you cut, keep your fingers on the tip of the tail as a safeguard.

Typical Westie!
Its double coat protects it from wind and weather, but because the dog does not molt naturally, its coat has to be trimmed regularly.

4. Trim the hair on the upper thighs without removing too much, but don't remove too little either, or the dog will appear to be wearing jodhpurs.

5. The hair on the back feet needs to be short and thick, but not too long. Using the scissors, clip the hair on the paws to give a rounded look.

6. The body hair on the abdomen should be left full and long. Cut the tips at an angle, with the hair in front slightly longer than that in back.

7. Trim the legs to look like thick, straight columns. Using the thinning shears, remove any long, protruding hair at the elbows.

8. Cut the hair on the front paws into a rounded shape.

9. Using the thinning shears, thin the hair on the shoulder blades as far as the elbows, and the hair at the side of the neck and below the head as far as the point where the forelegs begin. The transitions between the trimmed areas and the thinned areas have to be smooth and natural-looking. Leave the long hair between the forelegs. The front should appear straight.

10. The hair on the head should be dense and full. With the trimming knife or scissors, shorten it so that no parting is created. Cut the outer edge of the head in a U shape.

11. Clip the hair from the tips of the ears, so that about each ear is clear about one-third of the way down.

A properly trimmed Westie.

Index

Note: Numbers in **bold face** refer to photographs or drawings.

A

Accessories, 17–18
Accidents, 47
Acclimation
  car trip home with puppy, 20
  first days in new home, 20
  first few nights, 24
Agility, 38
Airline travel, 30
AKC registration number, 17
American Kennel Club, 10–11,
  50–51
Amino acids, 36
Appearance, 10
Aujesky's disease, 45
Automatic waterer, 17
Average daily requirements, 36

B

Barking, 28
Baths, 26
Begging, **16**
Behavior
  articulate language, 28
  body language, 28–29
Birth, 54
Bites, 47
Boarding kennels, 30
Body, 10
Body language, 28–29
Bones, 34–35
Breeders, 14–15
Breeding
  birth, 54–55
  development of puppies, 55

economics of, 50
false pregnancy, 52
feeding the puppies, 55
and female dogs, 51–52
and male dogs, 51
mating, 52
pregnancy, 52
regulations of, 50–51
responsibility for, 50
whelping box, 52–53
Breed standard, 10–11
Buying considerations, 12–19

C

Calcium supplement, 34, 55
Canned dog food, 34
Carbohydrates, 36
Car travel, 30
Character traits, 4
Charcoal, 46
Children, 4, **21**, **33**
Coat, 6, 11
  grooming, 26
  trimming, 26, 58–59
Collar, 17
Color, 11
"Come," 23
Commands
  "come," 23
  "phooey," 22–23
  "sit," 22
  "stay," 23
Commercial dog food, 33–34
Contract of sale, 17
Craniomandibular osteopathy, 45

D

Development, 55
Diarrhea, 37
Digestive system, 32
  upsets in, 37
Diseases, 11, 45. *See also*
  Illness; Preventive medicine
Drinking water, 34
Dry dog food, 34

E

Ears, 10
  care of, 27
  signals of, 28
Equipment, 17
Estrus, 51–52
Euthanasia, 31
Exercise, 4
Expenses, 12
Eyes, 10
  care of, 27

F

False pregnancy, 52
Fats, 36
Fatty acids, 36
Feeding
  old dog, 36
  overweight dog, 36–37
  place and time for, 32–33
  puppies, 33, 55
  rules for, 35
Feet, 11
  care of, 27
Females, 12–13, 51–52

Fetal membrane, 54
First aid
  accidents, 47
  bites, 47
  insect bites, 46–47
  kit for, 40
  paw cuts, 47
  poisoning, 46
First days/nights home, 24
Flea collars, 44
Fleas, 45
Flyball, 38–39
Food dish, 17
Front legs, 10
Full-grown dog, 13

G
Gestation period, 52
Grooming
  accessories for, 18
  coat, 26, 58–59
  ears, 27
  eyes, 27
  feet, 27
  teeth, 27
  trimming nails, 26
Growling, 28

H
Hazards, list of, 19
Heat, 51–52
Height, 4, 11
Hindquarters, 10–11
History of breed, 6–7
Hitting, 23
Housebreaking, 24–25
Howling, 28
Hunting instinct, **5**, 6

I
Illness
  first aid, 46–47
  medication administration, 42
  pulse, 42
  report to veterinarian, 42–43
  signs of, 40

temperature taking, 40, 42
Immunizations, 43–44
  schedule for, 43
Imprinting phase, 55
Insect bites, 46–47

K
Kibble, 34

L
Labor
  complications of, 54
  stages of, 54
Lactation, 55
Lactose, 34
Language, 28
Leash, 17
Leash breaking, 22
Life expectancy, 30

M
Males, 12–13, 51
Marking, 29, **29**
Mating, 52
Medication, administering, 42
Metabolism, 32
Milk, 34
Minerals, 36
Moist dog food, 34

N
Nails, trimming, 26
Neck, 10
Nose, 10
Nursing, 55
Nutrition
  appropriate, 32
  average daily requirements, 36
  bones, 34–35
  commercial dog food, 33–34
  digestive upsets, 37
  drinking water, 34
  home-prepared meals, 35–36
  for old dogs, 36
  for overweight dogs, 36–37
  for pregnant dogs, 52

for puppies, 33, 55
right amounts of, 32–33
rules for, 35

O
Obstacle course, 38
Old dog, 30–31
  nutrition for, 36
Origin of breed, 6–7
Other dogs, 6
Other pets, 14
Overweight dog, 36–37

P
Pack animals, 23
Parasites, 44–45
Paw cuts, 47
Pedigree, 17, 50–51
"Phooey," 22–23
Physical fitness, 38–39
Placenta, 54
Play, **13**
Poisoning, 46
Pork, 36, 45
Pregnancy, 52
  false, 52
  intervals between, 51
Pressure dressing, 47
Preventive medicine
  immunizations, 43–44
  parasites, 44–45
  worming, 44
Prey animals, 32
Protein, 35–36
Psychological development, 12
Pulse, taking, 42
Puppies, 13, **25**, **36**
  acclimation of, 20–25
  birth of, 54
  choosing, 14
  development of, 55
  feeding schedule, 17
  immunization schedule, 43
  nursing, 55
  nutrition for, 33, **37**, 55
  training, 22–23

worming schedule, 43
"Puppy mills," 15
Purchase price, 12

Q
Quarantine regulations, 29

R
Raw beef/pork, 36
Rawhide toys, 18
Reducing diet, 32, 36–37

S
Safety harness, 30
Scent marking, 29, **29**
Semimoist dog food, 34
Sexual receptivity period, 51
Shoulders, 10
Showers, 26
Show lead, 17
Shows
  how dogs are judged, 56, 58
  preparing for show ring, 58
  trimming coat before a show,
    58–59
  types of, 56
"Sit," 22
Skull, 10
Sleeping basket, 17
Sniffing, 29
Socialization phase, 22, 55
Sports, 38, **48–49**
"Stay," 23
Stubborness, 6, 23
Stud, 51
Submission, **24**
Suppositories, 42

T
Tail, 11
  signals of, 28–29
Tartar, 27
Teeth, 10
  care of, 27
Temperament, 10

Temperature, taking, 40, 42
Thermometers, 40
Ticks, 44–45
Tourniquet, 47
Toys, 17–18
Track the scent, 39
Training
  basic rules of, 23
  commands, 22–23
  housebreaking, 24–25
  leash breaking, 22
  for shows, 58
  staying alone, 23
Train travel, 30
Trimming
  coat, 26, 58–59
  nails, 26
Two dogs, 13–14

U
Umbilical cord, 54

V
Vacations, 29–30
  checklist for, 31
Vaccination certificate, 15
Veterinarian, 15, 31, **44**
  report to, 42–43
Vomiting, 37

W
Walking, 38
Water dish, 17
Weeping eyes, 27
Weight, 4
West Highland white terrier,
  8–9, 57
Whelping box, 53–54
Whimpering, 28
Wolves, 28, 32
Worming, 15, 44, 55
  schedule for, 43

Y
Yelping, 28

Useful Books

For further reading on this subject and related matter, consult the following books also published by Barron's Educational Series, Inc.

Health

Alderton, David: *The Dog Care Manual,* 1986.
Frye, Frederic: *First Aid for Your Dog,* 1987.
Klever, U.: *The Complete Book of Dog Care,* 1989.
Streitferdt, U.: *Healthy Dog, Happy Dog. A Complete Guide to Dog Diseases and Their Treatment,* 1994.

Education

Baer, T.: *Communicating with Your Dog,* 1989.
Baer, T.: *How to Teach Your Old Dog New Tricks,* 1991.
Ullman, H.J.: *The New Dog Handbook,* 1984.
Wrede, B.: *Civilizing Your Puppy,* 1992.

Useful Magazines

Terrier Type. Published eleven times a year.
Contact Dan Kiedrowski, Post Office Drawer A, La Honda, CA 94020. (415) 747-0549.
Westie Imprint. Published quarterly.
Contact Daphne Gentry, West Highland White Terrier Club of America, 604 Arlie Street, Richmond, VA 23226. (804) 288-7424.

Useful Addresses

American Boarding
  Kennel Association
  4574 Galley Road,
  Suite 400A
  Colorado Springs,
  Colorado 80915

American Kennel Club
  51 Madison Avenue
  New York, NY 10010
  (212) 696-8200

American Society for
  the Prevention of
  Cruelty to Animals
  (ASPCA)
  424 East 92 Street
  New York, NY 10128
  (212) 876-7700

Canadian Kennel Club
  2150 Bloor Street W.
  Toronto, Ontario
  M6 540 Canada

United Kennel Club
  100 East Kilgore Rd.
  Kalamazoo, MI 49001
  (616) 343-9020

Veterinary Pet
  Insurance
  1-800-USA-PETS
  In California:
  1-800-VIP-PETS

West Highland White
  Terrier Club of
  America
  5870 U.S. Highway 6
  Portage, IN 46368
  (219) 762-2903

Author and Collaborator

Ingrid Bolle-Kleinbub began breeding West Highland white terriers in 1977, under the name "Wild Bunch."

She was one of the first 40 Westie breeders in West Germany. From 1978 to 1990 she was editor-in-chief of the magazine *Der Terrier,* and from 1978 to 1985 she headed the Terrier Club of 1894 in Kelsterbach. In 1990 she opened a grooming salon for Westies. Since 1991 her articles on Westies have appeared regularly in the journal *Kleinhundewelt The World of Small Dogs.*

Christine Metzger has been a free-lance journalist since 1985, with numerous publications (books, newspapers, periodicals, radio).

The Photographers

Animal Photography/ Thompson, Willbie: inside front cover/page 1, pages 8/9, 13, 21, 24, 29 top, 29 bottom, 33, 37, 41, 44, 48/49, 53, back cover; Cogis/Amblin: page 32; Cogis/Lanceau: page 64/inside back cover; Cogis/Varin: page 29 middle; Cogis/Vedie: page 36; Foto Hermann: front cover; IPO: page 16; Jacana/Frederic: page 5; Jacana/Mero: page 17; Junior/Tüngler: page 20; Runge: pages 12, 40, 52, 57; Steimer: page 45; WAPI/Nicaise: pages 4, 25.

Source Note

The sections "How the Dog Owner Can Help" and "What the Veterinarian Needs to Know" [from chapter "What to Do If Your Westie Gets Sick"] were written by Dr. Uwe Streitferdt.

Important Notes

This Barron's pet owner's manual deals with the acquisition and care of West Highland white terriers. The author and the publishers believe it is important to point out that the guidelines for pet owners presented in this book apply primarily to normally developed young dogs from reputable breeders, that is, healthy dogs with excellent characters. If you adopt a full-grown animal, you need to realize that it has already been substantially influenced by human contacts. Look it over first with a critical eye, and watch how it responds to people. Meet the previous owner, if possible. If the dog comes from an animal shelter, someone there may be able to give you information about the dog's background and traits. Some dogs, because of bad experiences with humans, behave in an unnatural way, and they may even have a tendency to bite. These dogs should be adopted only by dog owners with plenty of experience. Even with well-trained and carefully supervised dogs, there is a chance that they will damage other people's property or even cause accidents. It is in your own interest to have adequate insurance coverage; in any case, I strongly urge that you purchase a dog liability insurance policy.

Make sure that your dog gets all the necessary immunizations and worming treatments (see page 43); otherwise, your health and you pet's are at substantial risk. Some diseases and parasites are communicable to humans (see pages 43 and 44). If your dog shows some symptoms of illness, it is essential to consult a veterinarian. When in doubt, see your own physician and tell him or her that you keep a dog.

Acknowledgments

I would like to thank my daughter, Daniela, her friend Margit Kühler, and my husband, Rudolf, for their assistance; Dr. Sabine Schall and Dr. Horst Schall, veterinarians from Ludwigshafen, for the many years of excellent care they have given my Westies; and our "vacation fairy," Susanne Meyer.

The U.S. editor gratefully acknowledges the valuable assistance provided by Ms. Susan Marie Napady, Secretary of the West Highland White Terrier Club of America.

© Copyright 1993 by Gräfe und Unzer GmbH, Munich.
The title of the German book is *Der Westie. West Highland White Terrier.*
Translated from the German by Kathleen Luft.
First English language edition published in 1994 by Barron's Educational Series, Inc.
English translation © Copyright 1994 by Barron's Educational Series, Inc.

Address all inquiries to:
Barron's Educational Series, Inc.
250 Wireless Boulevard
Hauppauge, New York 11788

Library of Congress Catalog Card No. 94-71600

International Standard Book No. 0-8120-1950-4

Printed in Hong Kong
567   9927   98